THE DECOLONIZATION OF AMERICA

TEXT AND COLLAGES BY STEFFEN ZILLIG

WIRKLICHKEIT BOOKS • AKV BERLIN

The collages are sourced from the following German-language original copies: *Andy Morgan: Abenteuer in Manhattan* by Hermann and Michel Greg *Andy Morgan: Durch die Flammenhölle von Caranoa* by Hermann and Michel Greg *Andy Morgan: Pest an Bord* by Hermann and Michel Greg *Andy Morgan: Eine Frau wie Dynamit* by Edouard Aidans and Michel Greg *Andy Morgan: Grünes Gift* by Edouard Aidans and Michel Greg *Antares: Episode 1* by Leo *Barry Lan: Hüter meines Schlafes* by Jeanine Rahir and Renée Rahir *Die Bokanovsky Erzählungen* by Michael Musal and Benno Samuel *Brüsel* by François Schuiten and Benoit Peeters *Chancen* by Horacio Altuna *Convoi: Gefangen im System* by Thierry Smolderen and Philippe Gauckler *Convoi: Das Spiel der Spiele* by Thierry Smolderen and Philippe Gauckler *Convoi: Stereopolis* by Thierry Smolderen and Philippe Gauckler *Cyann – Tochter der Sterne: Der Sterbende Planet* by François Bourgeon and Claude Lacroix *Dan Cooper: Die Männer mit den goldenen Flügeln* by Albert Weinberg *Dragstor: Die Sonnenbombe* by Julio Bosch and Hansjürgen Meyer *Die Farbe der Wildnis: Mihalis* by Ugolino Cossu and Guiseppe Ferrandino *Das Geschichtsbuch – Teil 1: bis 1914* by Annika Elmquist, Gittan Jönsson, Ann Marie Langemar and Pål Rydberg *Gil Saint-André: Eine seltsame Entführung* by Jean-Charles Kraehn and Sylvain Vallée *Gord: Auge um Auge …* by Christian Denayer and Franz Drappier *Gord: Planet der Geächteten* by Christian Denayer and Franz Drappier *Gregorka im 21. Jahrhundert: Der Plan* by Martin Frei *Helen und andere Liebesgeschichten* by Bob de Groot and Philippe Francq *Der Ideenhändler 3: Die Suche nach dem Sternensäer* by Philippe Berthet and André Cossu *Inio: Snow-City* by Dirk Tonn *Jenseits der Grenze* by Francois Schuiten and Benoit Peeters *Jeremiah: Afromerica* by Hermann *Jeremiah: Aufstand der Tagelöhner* by Hermann *Jeremiah: Falsche Hoffnungen* by Hermann *Jeremiah: Julius und Romea* by Hermann *Der Joker: Der Alte von Brooklyn* by Dany and Jean van Hamme *Kelly Green: Gefangen im Eis Alaskas* by Stan Drake and Leonard Starr *Lady S: Auf dein Wohl Suzie!* by Jean van Hamme and Philippe Aymond *Lady S: Falsches Spiel* by Jean van Hamme and Philippe Aymond *Lady S: Ein Maulwurf in Washington* by Jean van Hamme and Philippe Aymond *Largo Winch: Gruppe W* by Philippe Francq and Jean van Hamme *Menschliche Überreste* by P. Craig Russell and Clive Barker *Mondbasis Alpha 1: Planet der Riesen-Armeisen* by Cardona and Fariñas *Negalyod* by Vincent Perriot *Die Pforten in die Vergangenheit* by Rodolphe and Ferrandez *Rael: Im Schatten der Sonne* by Colin Wilson *Scarlett Dream: Zwei Schritte zur Hölle* by Robert Gigi and Claude Moliterni *Die Träume des Caza* by Caza *Die Türme von Bos-Maury: Williams Irrweg* by Hermann *Der Turm* by François Schuiten and Benoit Peeters *Der Zyklus der zwei Horizonte: Anna* by Pierre Makyo and Christian Rossi

1. Edition 2021
Original Edition
Jointly published by
Wirklichkeit Books & AKV Berlin

Text and collages: Steffen Zillig
Translation: Ben Rosenthal
Proofreading: Kim Wrigley and Nicholas Tammens
Design: JMMP – Julian Mader, Max Prediger
Print: Memminger MedienCentrum

Supported by Hans-Böckler-Stiftung

wirklichkeitbooks.com
akvberlin.com

ISBN: 978-3-948200-07-7

Some Euro-Americans

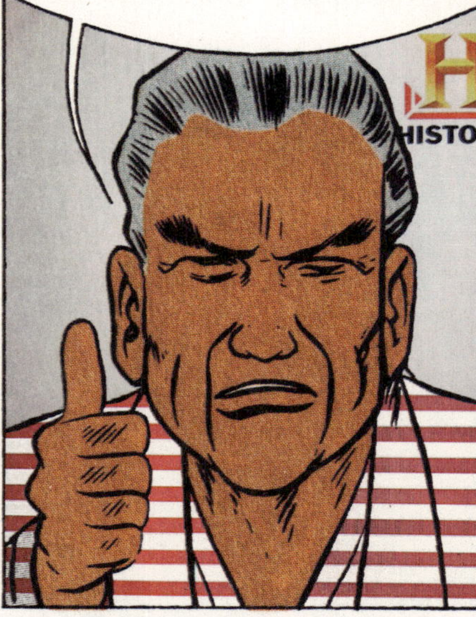

Cristóbal's enthusiasm makes up for his lack of honesty. A petty criminal, he used fake credit points to fraudulently obtain a ticket for remigration. However, he made many of his fellow travelers excited for a new beginning in the old world.

Gary Knopp isn't merely the narrator of this illustrated story, he is also the face of the historical program of the same name that airs on "African Prime". Knopp performed great services to cultural mediation and to the integration of a self-confident Euro-American identity in Africa.

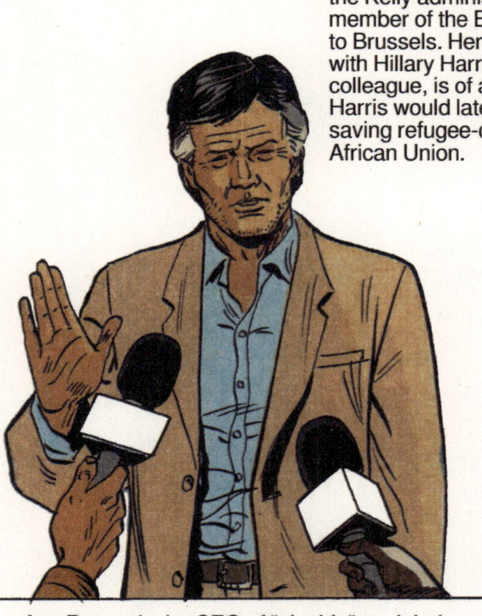

Angelina Colani is a junior consultant to the Kelly administration. She serves as a member of the Euro-American delegation to Brussels. Her long-term relationship with Hillary Harris, an African-American colleague, is of a more private character. Harris would later on negotiate the life-saving refugee-deal with the West African Union.

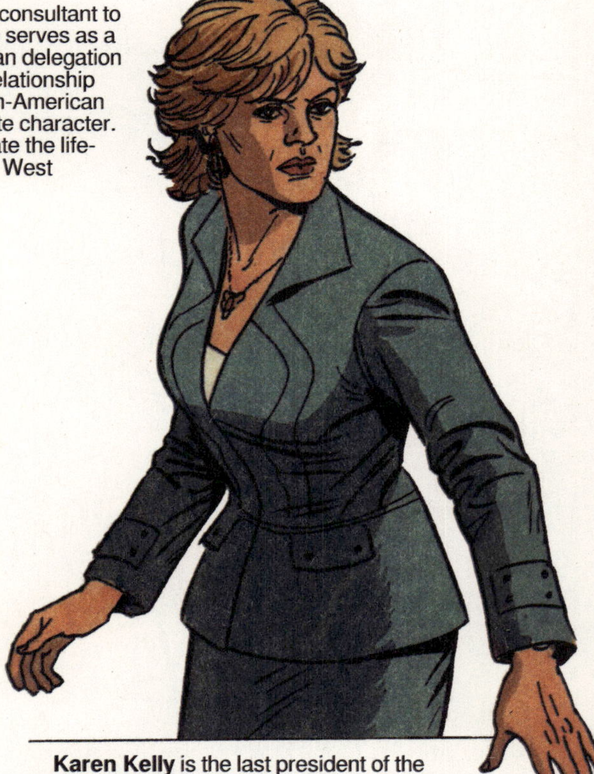

Joe Pesos is the CEO of "glooble", a global economic platform. In this role, he promotes the diversification of the company's salary structure. A sympathetic gun enthusiast and leisure time billionaire, Pesos advises the Kelly administration on the information campaign surrounding geographical decolonization.

Karen Kelly is the last president of the United States of America. Kelly is widely recognized for her pragmatism und crisis management skills. Her powerful speech on geographical decolonization ranks among the milestones of charismatic rhetoric in global politics.

They set sail on a frosty spring morning. Cargo boats and liners had formed a convoy. Cristóbal was on a boat carrying Andalusian, Breton and Frisian clusters. It felt like a big family outing. Members of various gene pools told fantastic stories about their distant homelands, to which they were heading.

They were the last ones to leave. Euphoric tweets of those who had remigrated to Africa and Greater China inspired them with the hope that they would be empraced by Europe just as warmly.

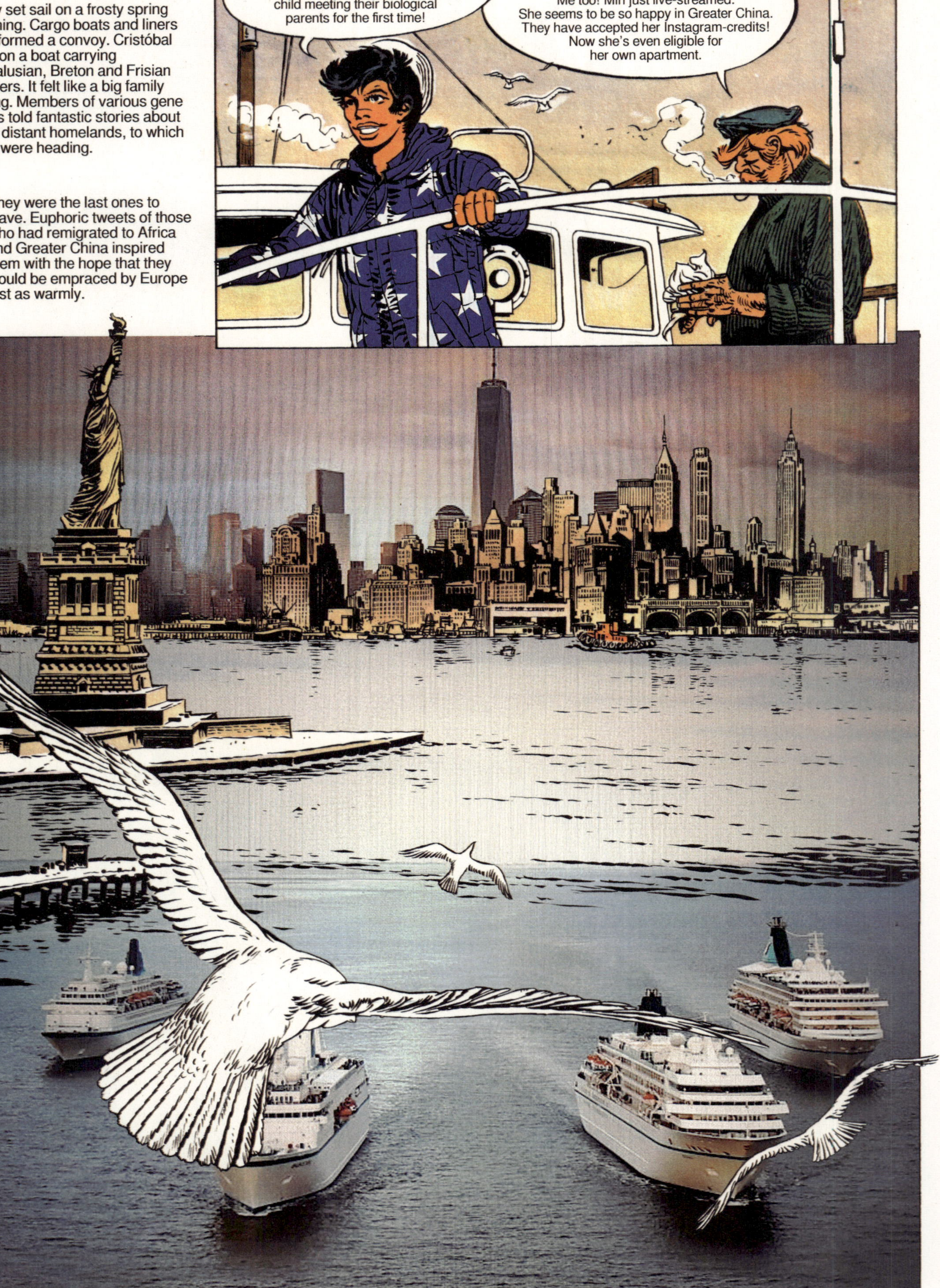

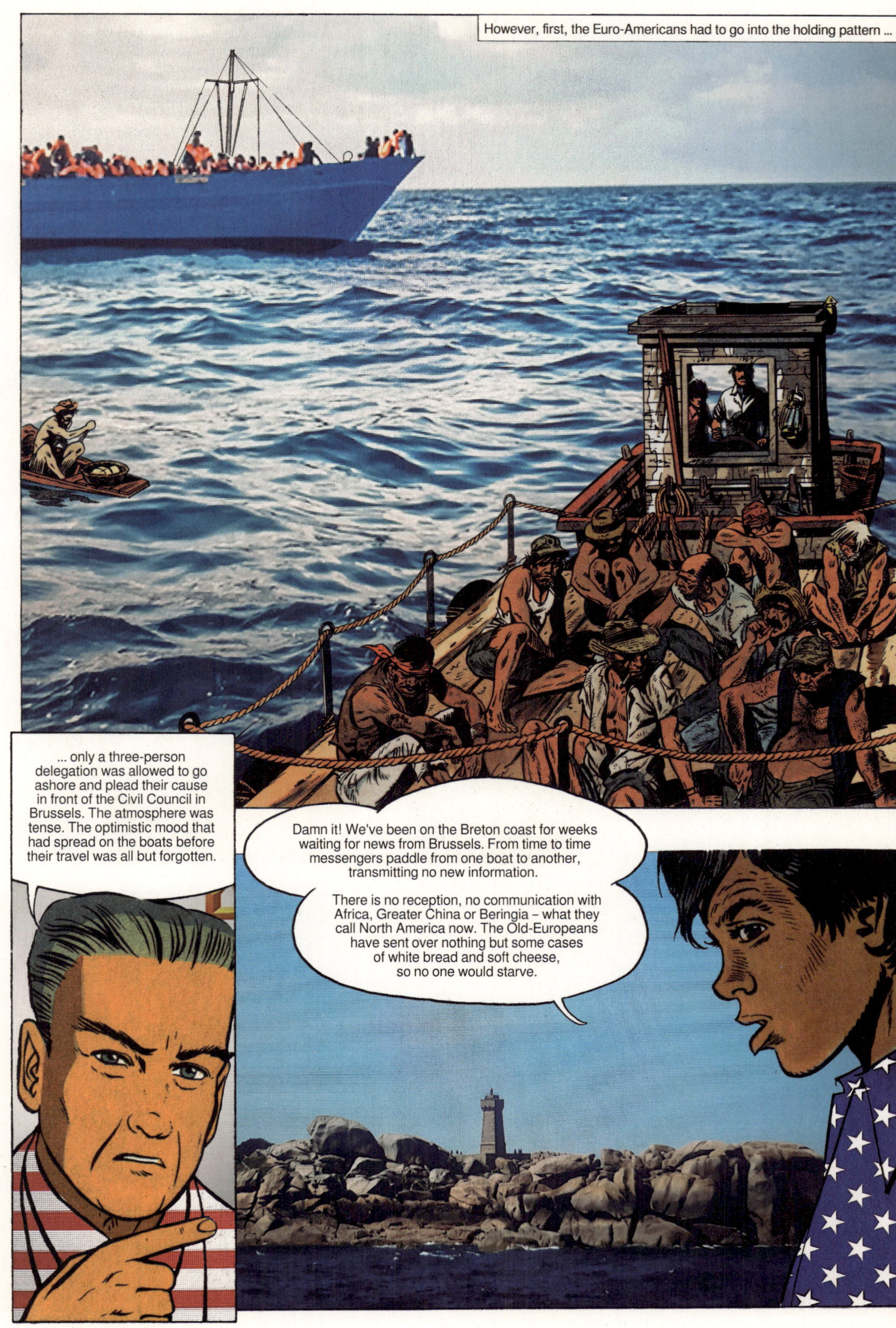

However, first, the Euro-Americans had to go into the holding pattern ...

... only a three-person delegation was allowed to go ashore and plead their cause in front of the Civil Council in Brussels. The atmosphere was tense. The optimistic mood that had spread on the boats before their travel was all but forgotten.

Damn it! We've been on the Breton coast for weeks waiting for news from Brussels. From time to time messengers paddle from one boat to another, transmitting no new information.

There is no reception, no communication with Africa, Greater China or Beringia – what they call North America now. The Old-Europeans have sent over nothing but some cases of white bread and soft cheese, so no one would starve.

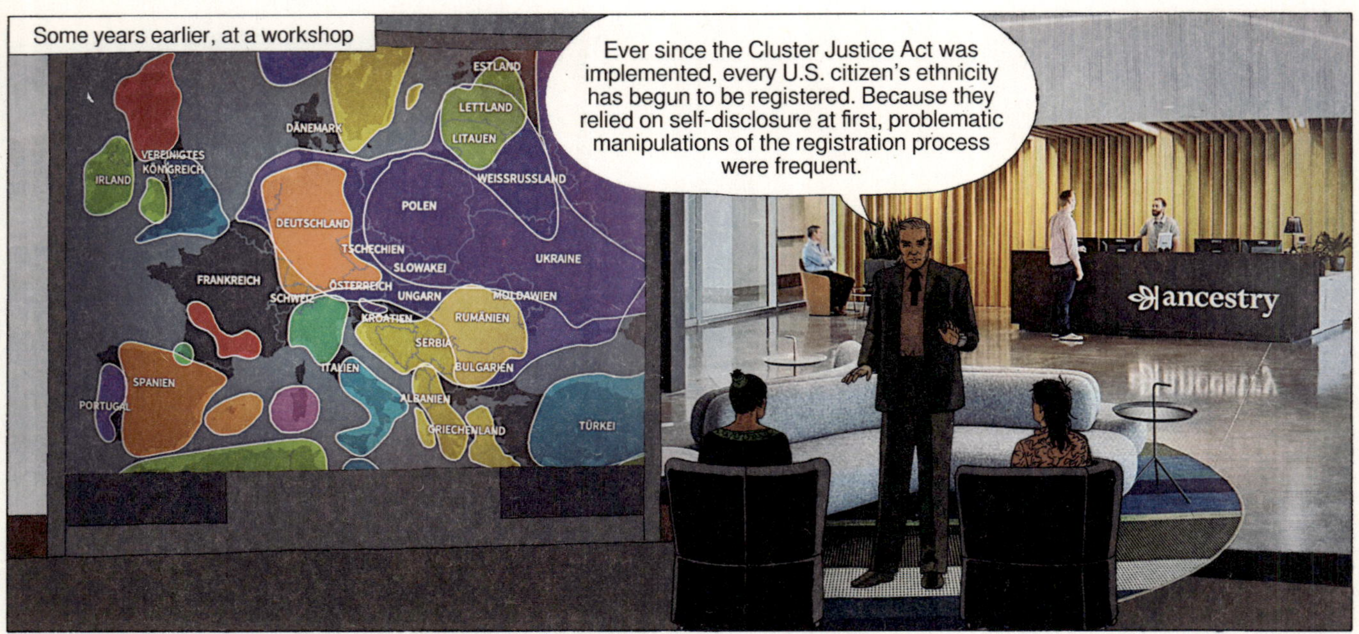

Some years earlier, at a workshop
Ever since the Cluster Justice Act was implemented, every U.S. citizen's ethnicity has begun to be registered. Because they relied on self-disclosure at first, problematic manipulations of the registration process were frequent.
VEREINIGTES KÖNIGREICH
IRLAND
DÄNEMARK
ESTLAND
LETTLAND
LITAUEN
WEISSRUSSLAND
POLEN
DEUTSCHLAND
TSCHECHIEN
SLOWAKEI
UKRAINE
FRANKREICH
SCHWEIZ
ÖSTERREICH
UNGARN
MOLDAWIEN
KROATIEN
RUMÄNIEN
SERBIA
ITALIEN
BULGARIEN
SPANIEN
ALBANIEN
PORTUGAL
GRIECHENLAND
TÜRKEI
ancestry

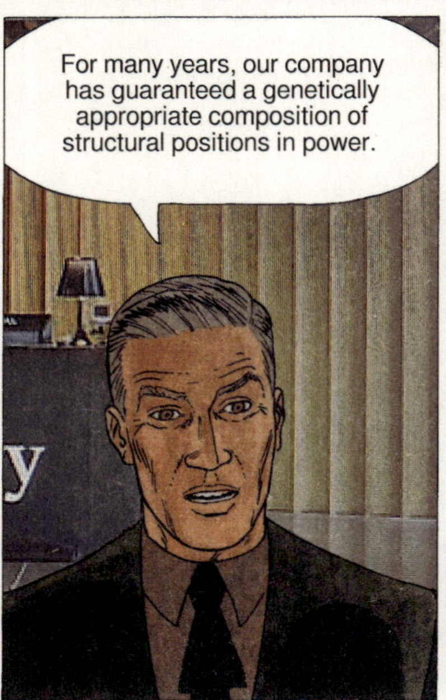

For many years, our company has guaranteed a genetically appropriate composition of structural positions in power.

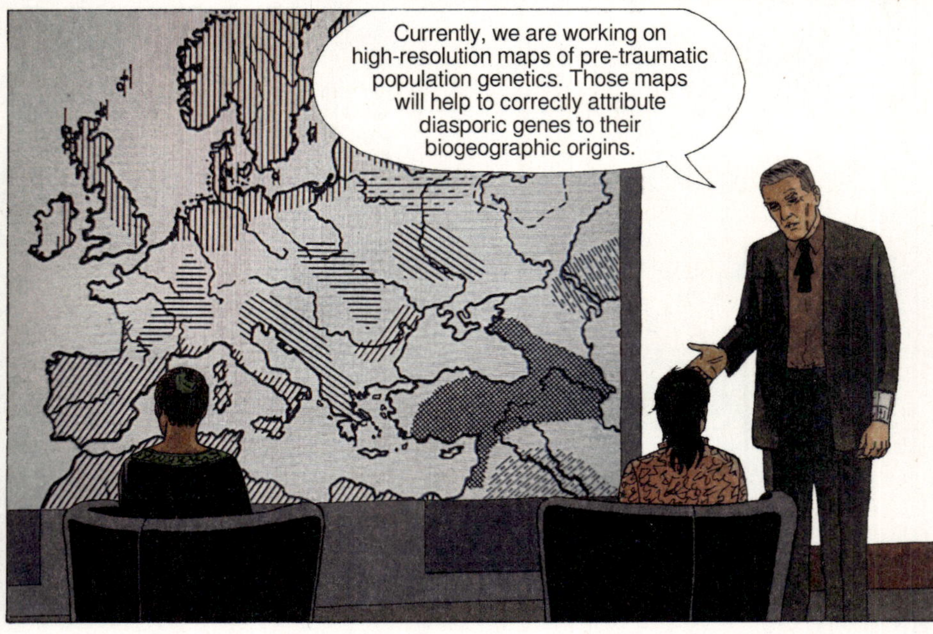

Currently, we are working on high-resolution maps of pre-traumatic population genetics. Those maps will help to correctly attribute diasporic genes to their biogeographic origins.

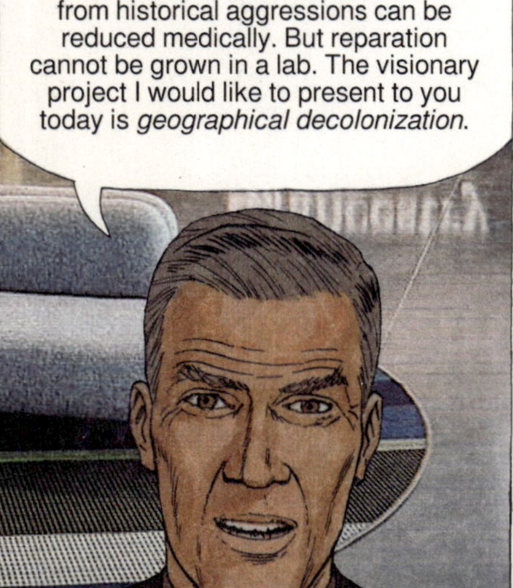

While today, epigenetic impairments from historical aggressions can be reduced medically. But reparation cannot be grown in a lab. The visionary project I would like to present to you today is geographical decolonization.

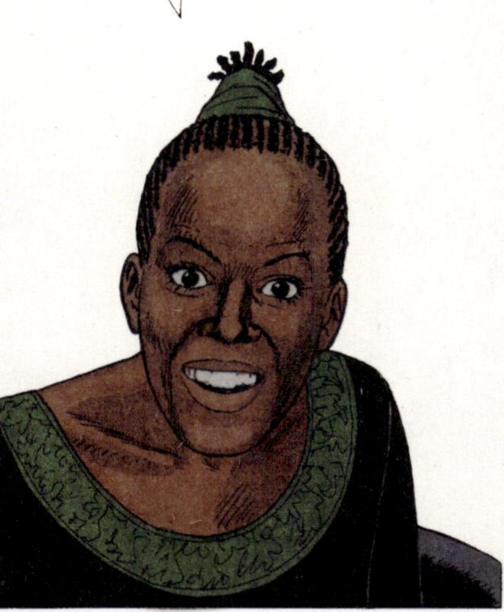

Wow!
Just wow!

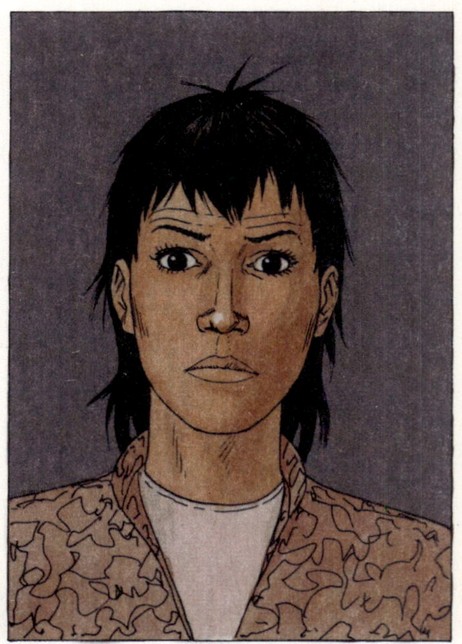

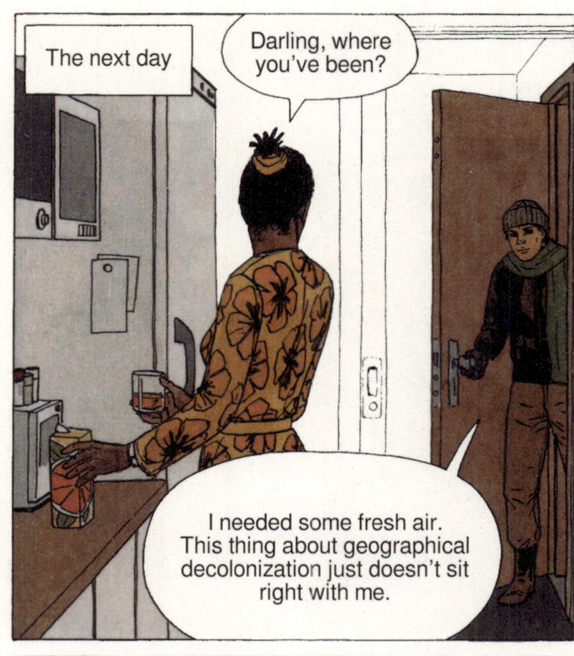

The next day
Darling, where you've been?
I needed some fresh air. This thing about geographical decolonization just doesn't sit right with me.

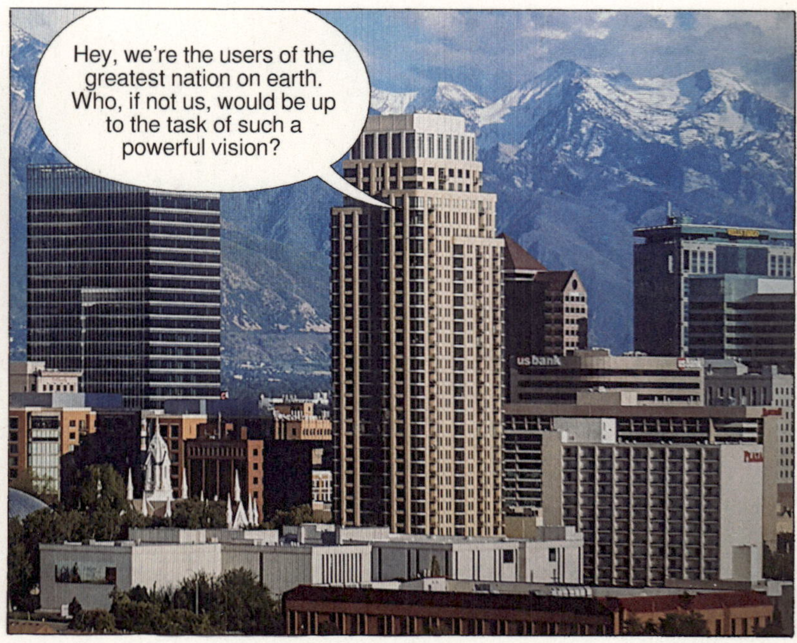

Hey, we're the users of the greatest nation on earth. Who, if not us, would be up to the task of such a powerful vision?

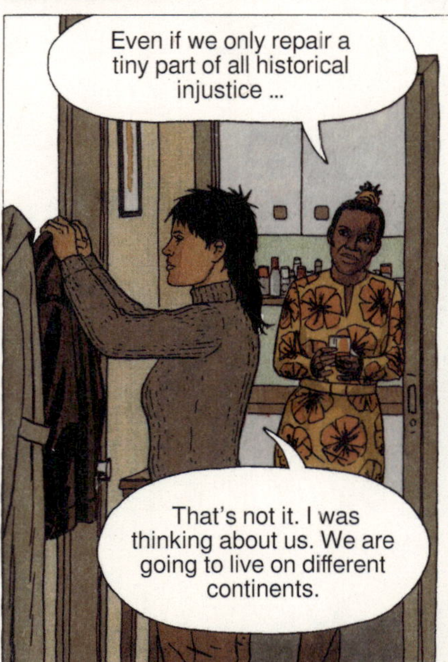

Even if we only repair a tiny part of all historical injustice …
That's not it. I was thinking about us. We are going to live on different continents.

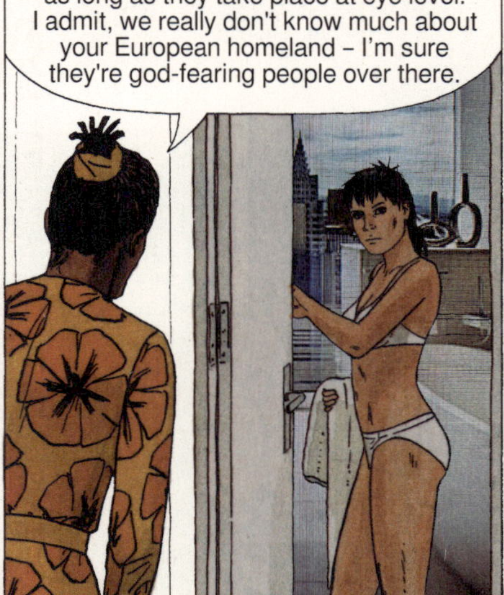

Mutual visits will still be allowed though, as long as they take place at eye level. I admit, we really don't know much about your European homeland – I'm sure they're god-fearing people over there.

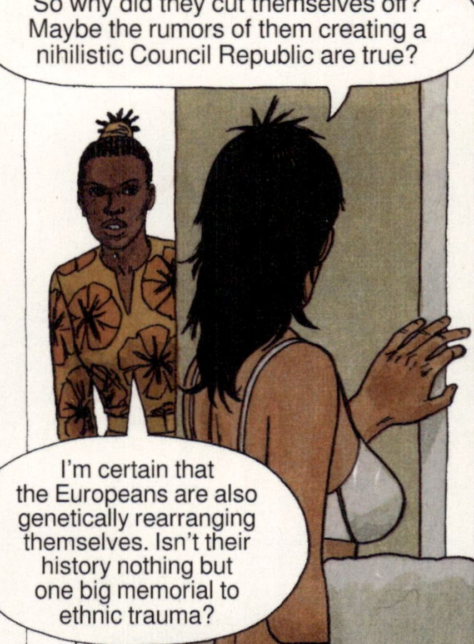

So why did they cut themselves off? Maybe the rumors of them creating a nihilistic Council Republic are true?
I'm certain that the Europeans are also genetically rearranging themselves. Isn't their history nothing but one big memorial to ethnic trauma?

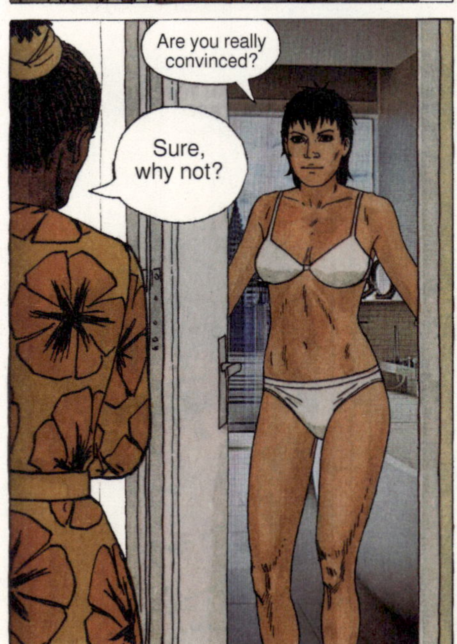

Are you really convinced?
Sure, why not?

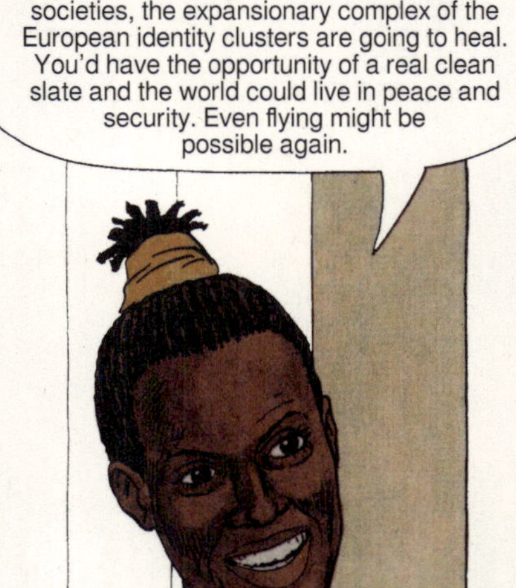

As soon as the biogeographic populations reintegrate into their respective societies, the expansionary complex of the European identity clusters are going to heal. You'd have the opportunity of a real clean slate and the world could live in peace and security. Even flying might be possible again.

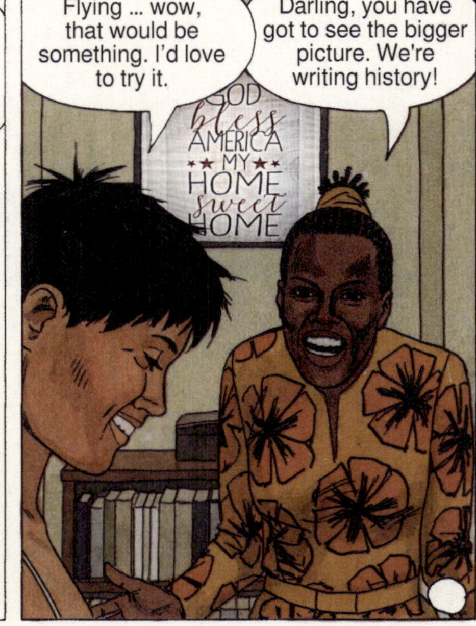

Flying … wow, that would be something. I'd love to try it.
Darling, you have got to see the bigger picture. We're writing history!
GOD bless AMERICA MY HOME sweet HOME

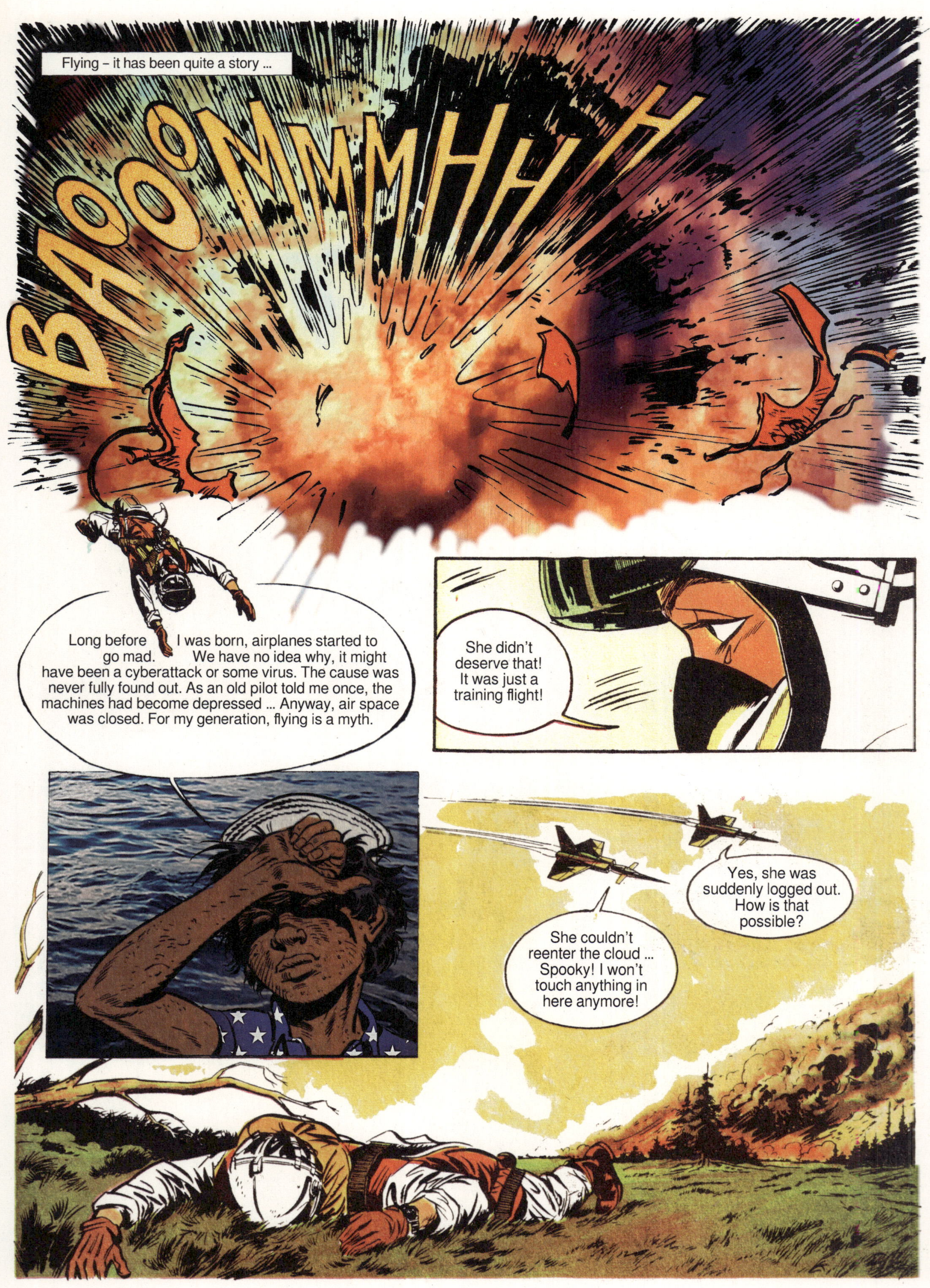

Flying – it has been quite a story ...
BAOOMMMHH
Long before I was born, airplanes started to go mad. We have no idea why, it might have been a cyberattack or some virus. The cause was never fully found out. As an old pilot told me once, the machines had become depressed ... Anyway, air space was closed. For my generation, flying is a myth.
She didn't deserve that! It was just a training flight!
She couldn't reenter the cloud ... Spooky! I won't touch anything in here anymore!
Yes, she was suddenly logged out. How is that possible?

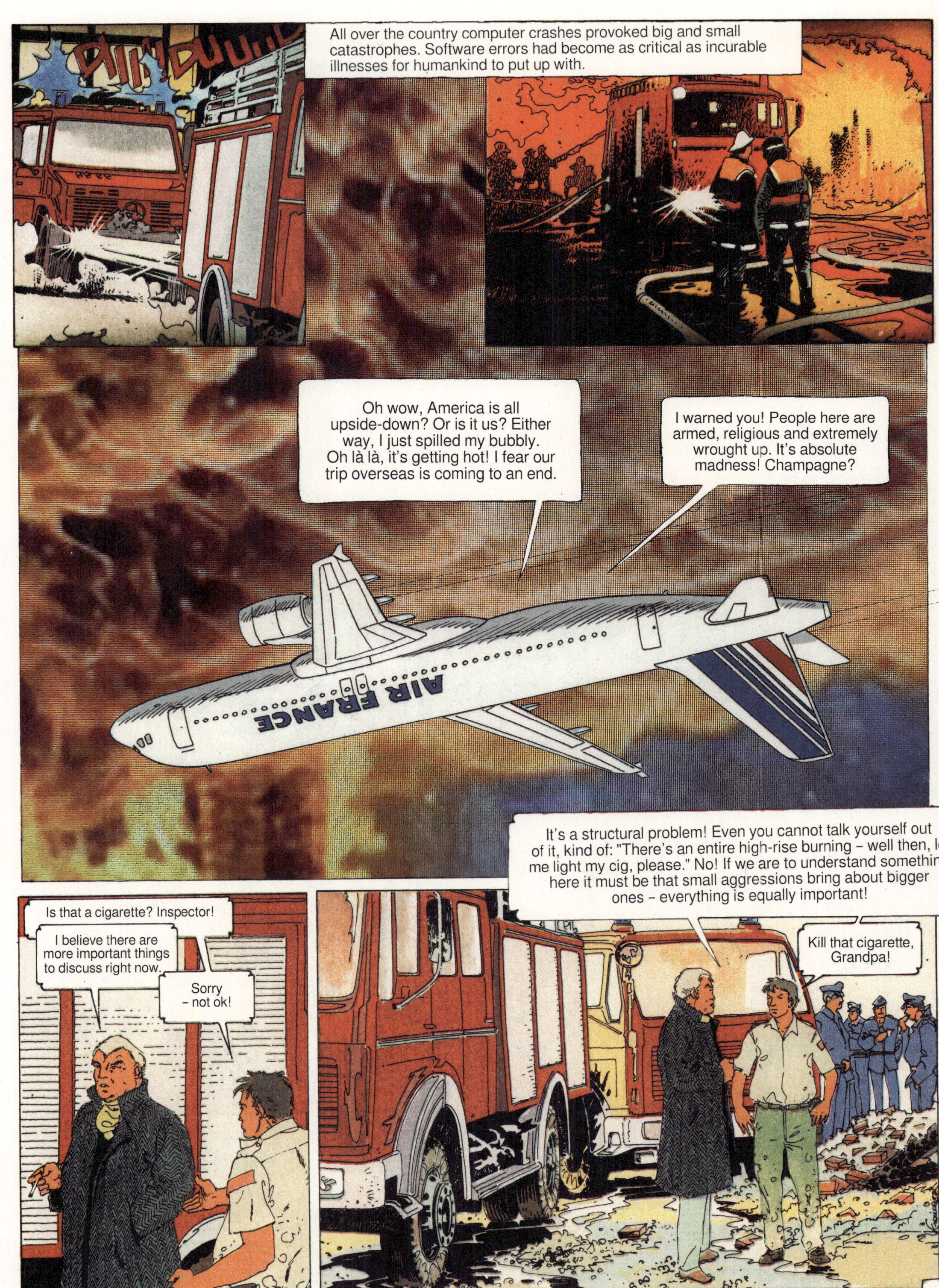

All over the country computer crashes provoked big and small catastrophes. Software errors had become as critical as incurable illnesses for humankind to put up with.

Oh wow, America is all upside-down? Or is it us? Either way, I just spilled my bubbly. Oh là là, it's getting hot! I fear our trip overseas is coming to an end.

I warned you! People here are armed, religious and extremely wrought up. It's absolute madness! Champagne?

AIR FRANCE

It's a structural problem! Even you cannot talk yourself out of it, kind of: "There's an entire high-rise burning – well then, let me light my cig, please." No! If we are to understand something here it must be that small aggressions bring about bigger ones – everything is equally important!

Is that a cigarette? Inspector!

I believe there are more important things to discuss right now.

Sorry – not ok!

Kill that cigarette, Grandpa!

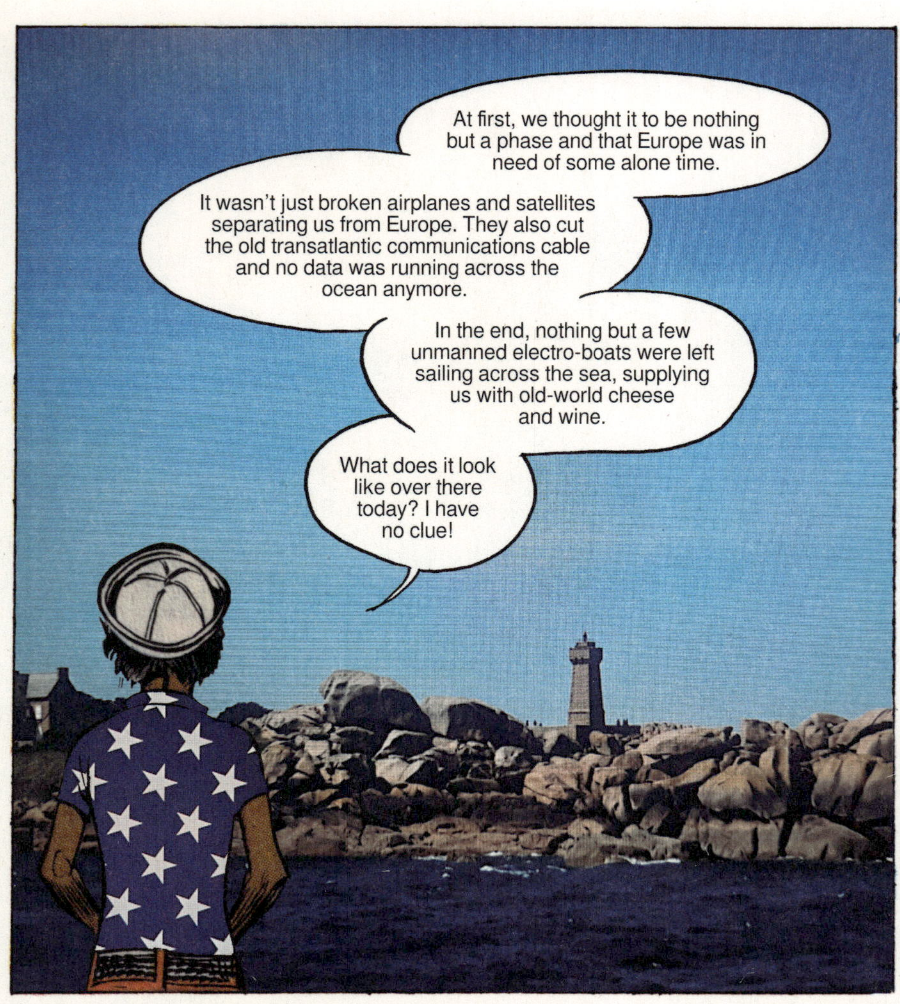

At first, we thought it to be nothing but a phase and that Europe was in need of some alone time.
It wasn't just broken airplanes and satellites separating us from Europe. They also cut the old transatlantic communications cable and no data was running across the ocean anymore.
In the end, nothing but a few unmanned electro-boats were left sailing across the sea, supplying us with old-world cheese and wine.
What does it look like over there today? I have no clue!

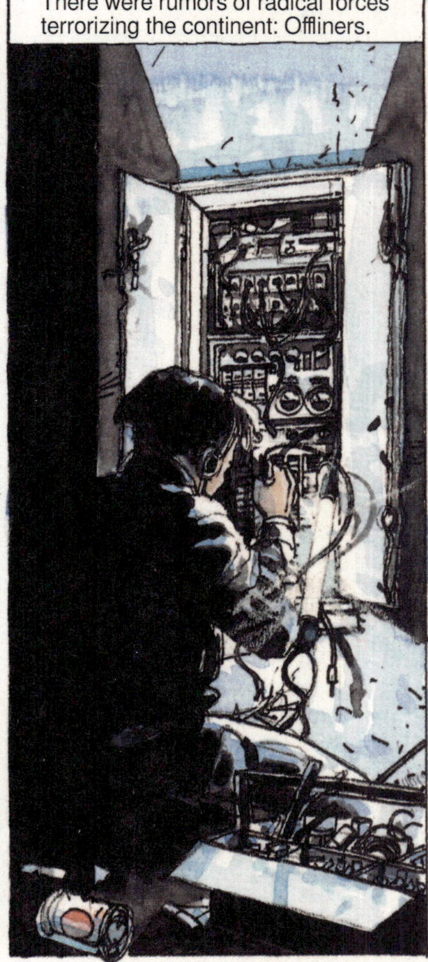

There were rumors of radical forces terrorizing the continent: Offliners.

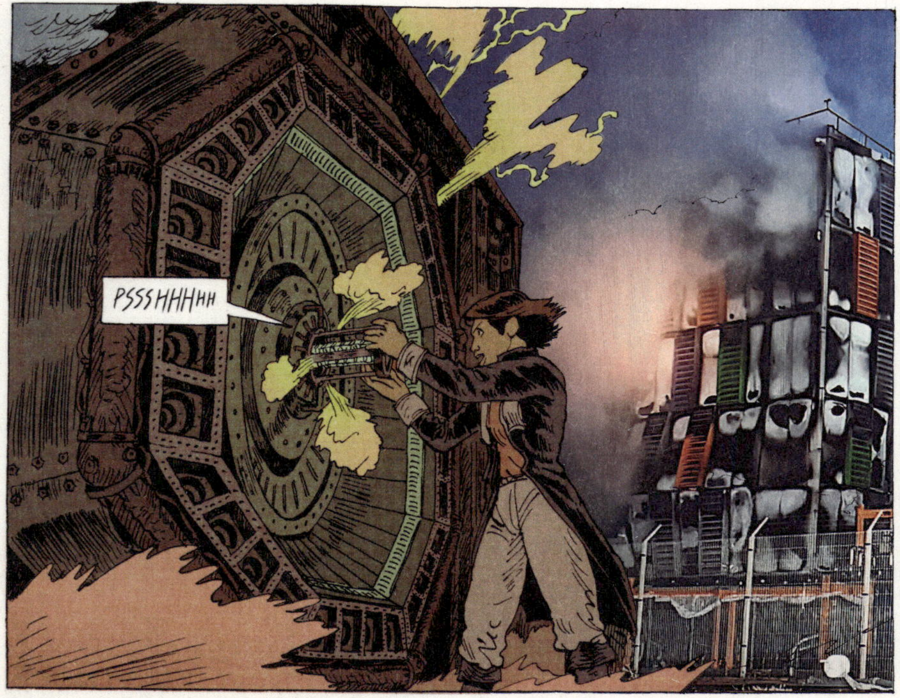

PSSSHHHHH

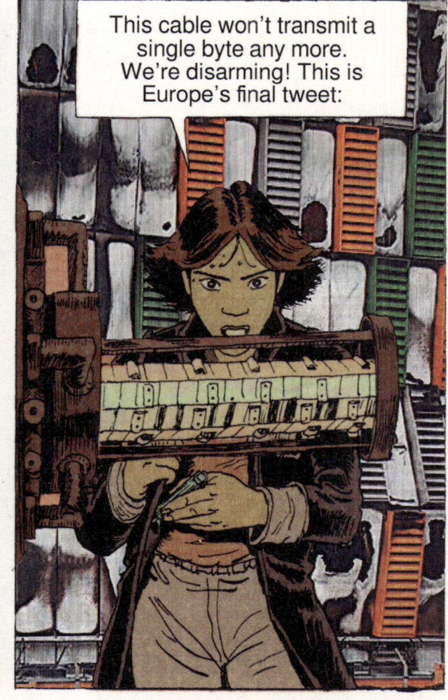

This cable won't transmit a single byte any more. We're disarming! This is Europe's final tweet:

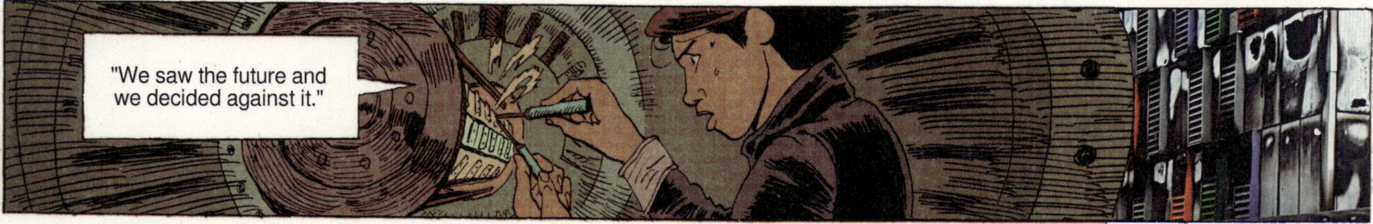

"We saw the future and we decided against it."

The Americans didn't mourn Europe for too long. It was the progress made internally which kept the country's users in its grip. Ardent measures were being taken for the establishment of a psycho-social balance between individual identity clusters.

Background analysis of genetic sequences and digital behavioral patterns allowed for a proper classification of the users. Platforms installed highly sensitive awareness-measuring devices. Those devices calculated behavioral irritations within a cluster and soothed them with activist conformity incentives.

Free preventive treatment for problematic hereditary lines was made mandatory. At least, it could ease the symptomatic of structural dullness by carefully implementing epigenetic corrections.

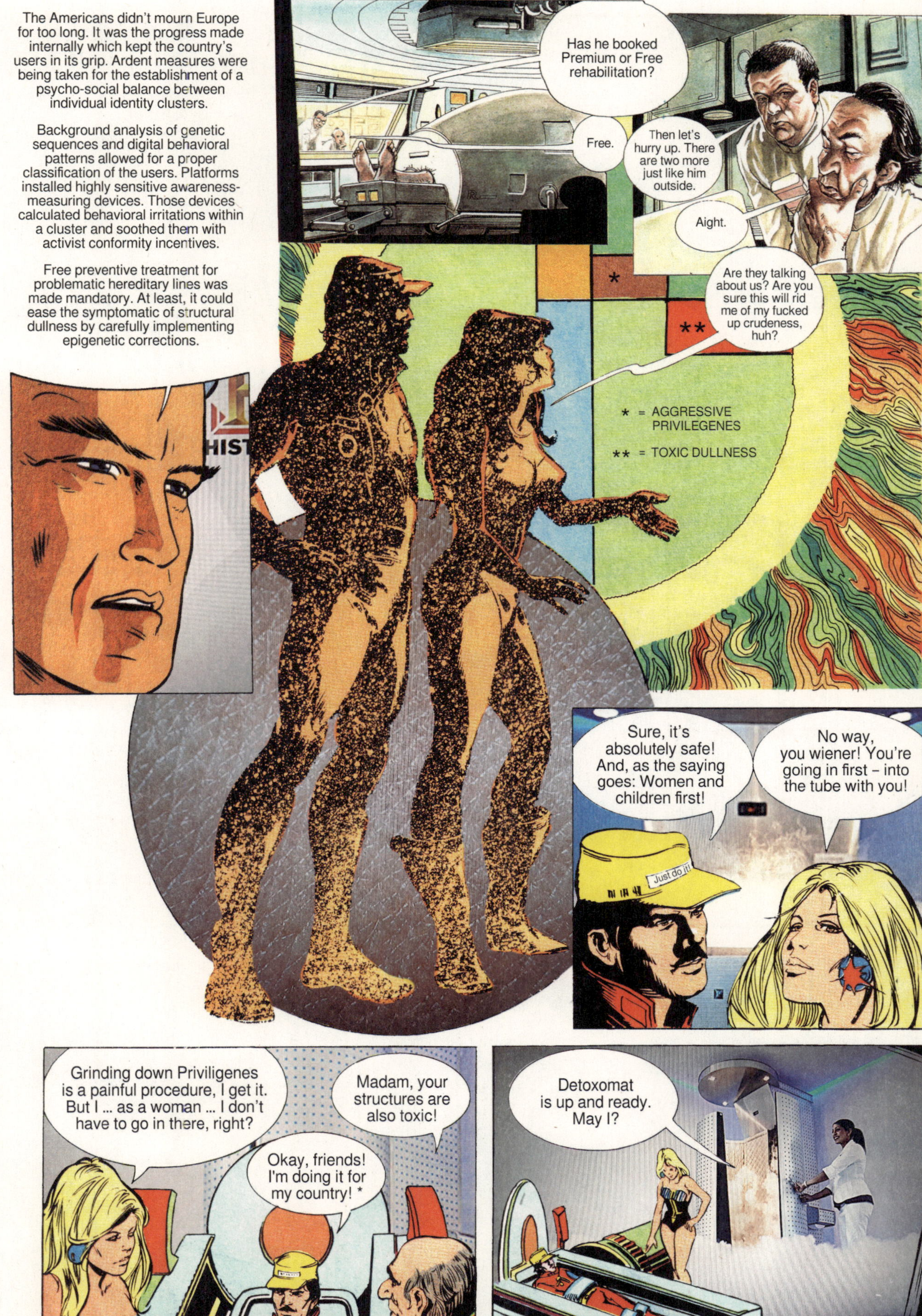

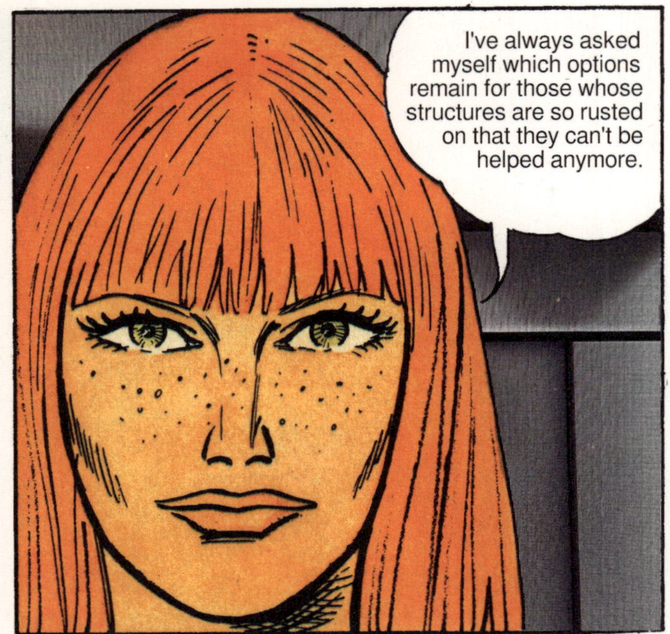

I've always asked myself which options remain for those whose structures are so rusted on that they can't be helped anymore.

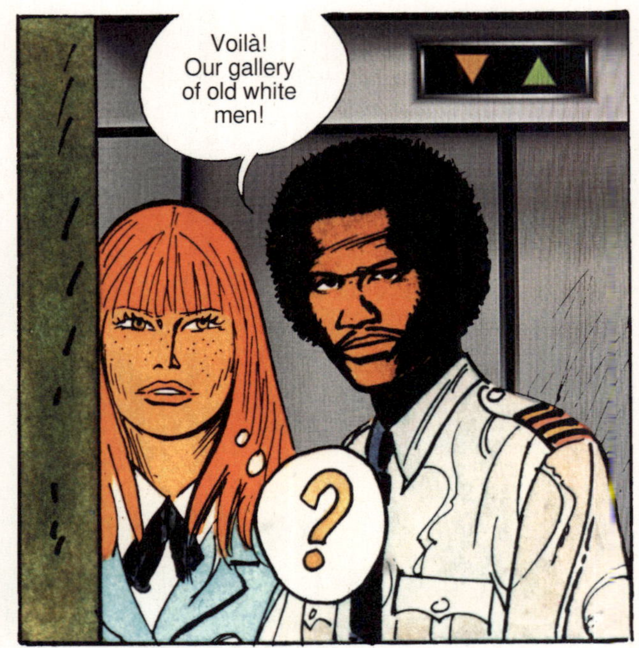

Voilà! Our gallery of old white men!
?

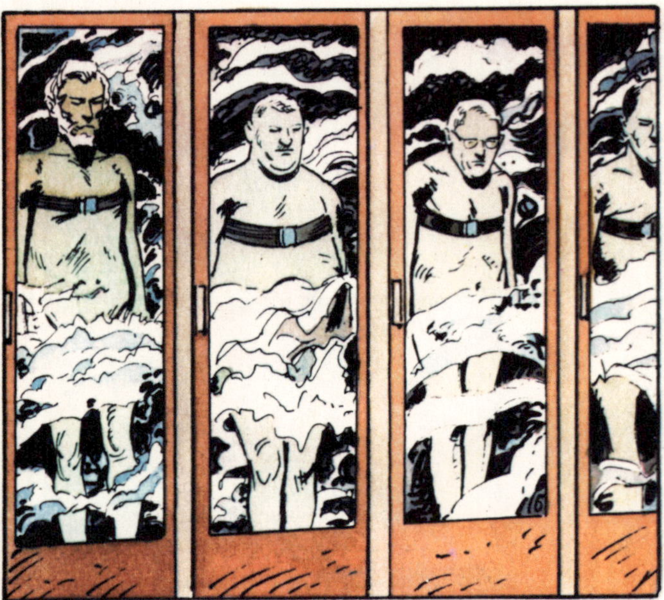

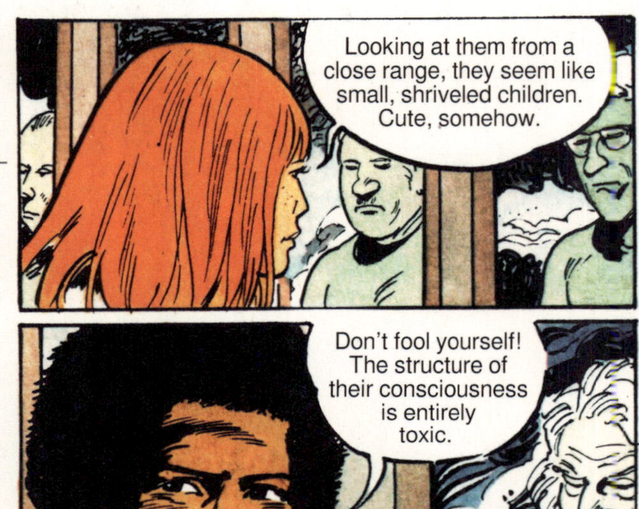

Looking at them from a close range, they seem like small, shriveled children. Cute, somehow.
Don't fool yourself! The structure of their consciousness is entirely toxic.

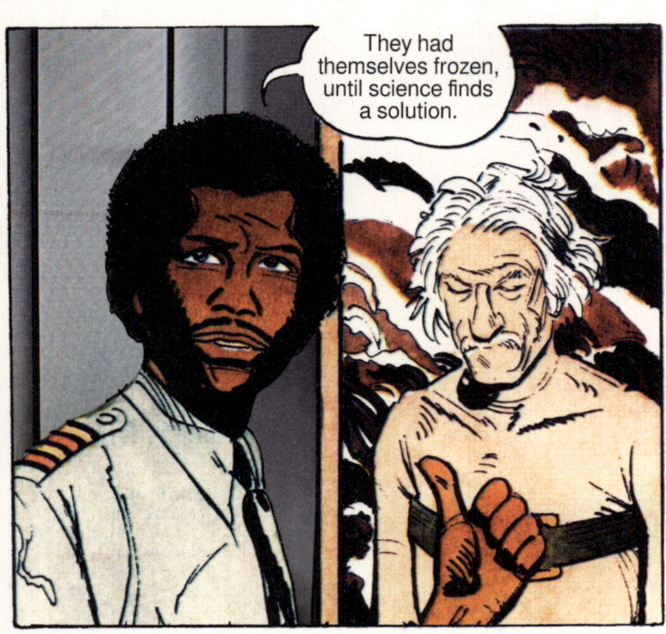

They had themselves frozen, until science finds a solution.

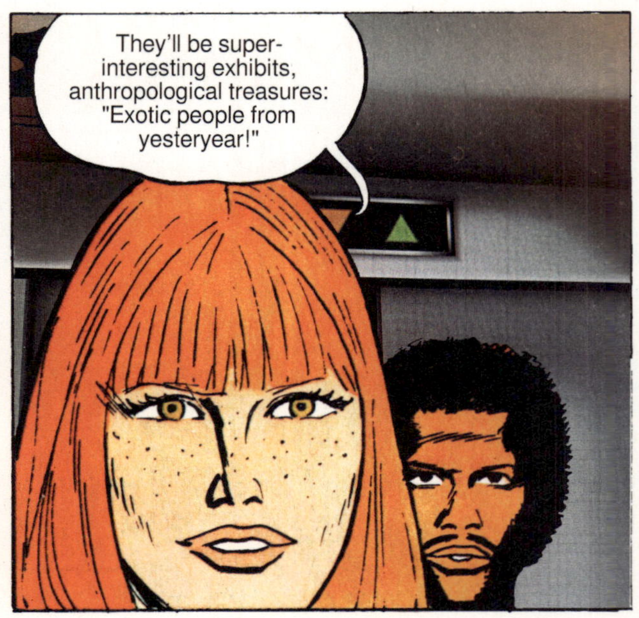

They'll be super-interesting exhibits, anthropological treasures: "Exotic people from yesteryear!"

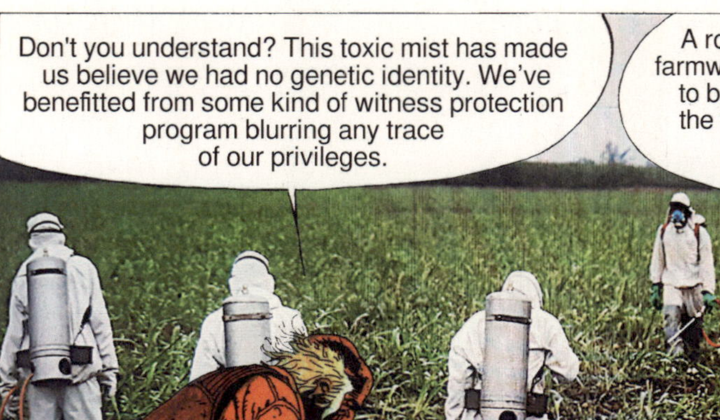

Don't you understand? This toxic mist has made us believe we had no genetic identity. We've benefitted from some kind of witness protection program blurring any trace of our privileges.

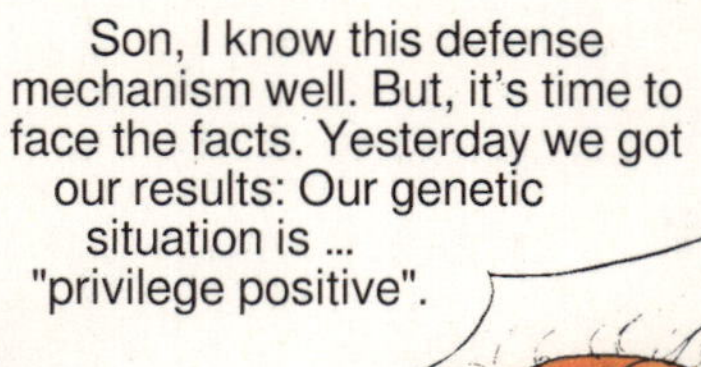

A rotten fourth-generation farmworker who also happens to be a severe alcoholic in the third generation. What privileges are you talking about?

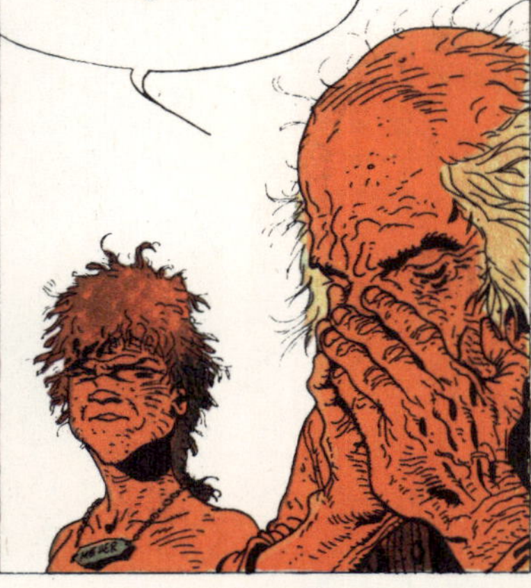

Son, I know this defense mechanism well. But, it's time to face the facts. Yesterday we got our results: Our genetic situation is … "privilege positive".

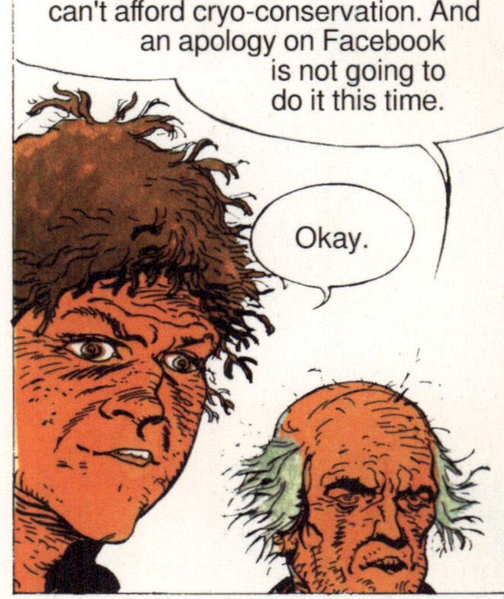

The legacy of our kin is a disaster, "inoperable". For too long we ignored it all, inventing new identities and hiding in false clusters … Son, we can't afford cryo-conservation. And an apology on Facebook is not going to do it this time.
Okay.

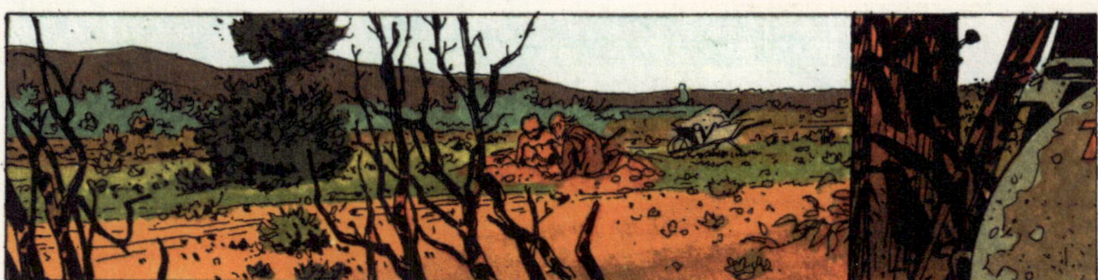

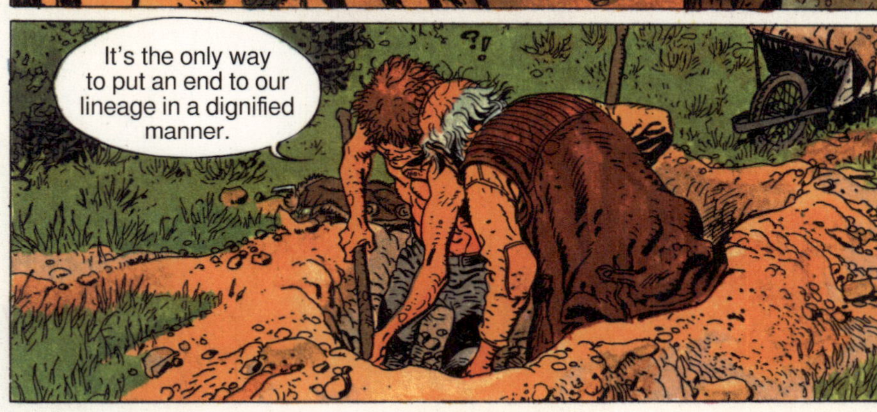

It's the only way to put an end to our lineage in a dignified manner.

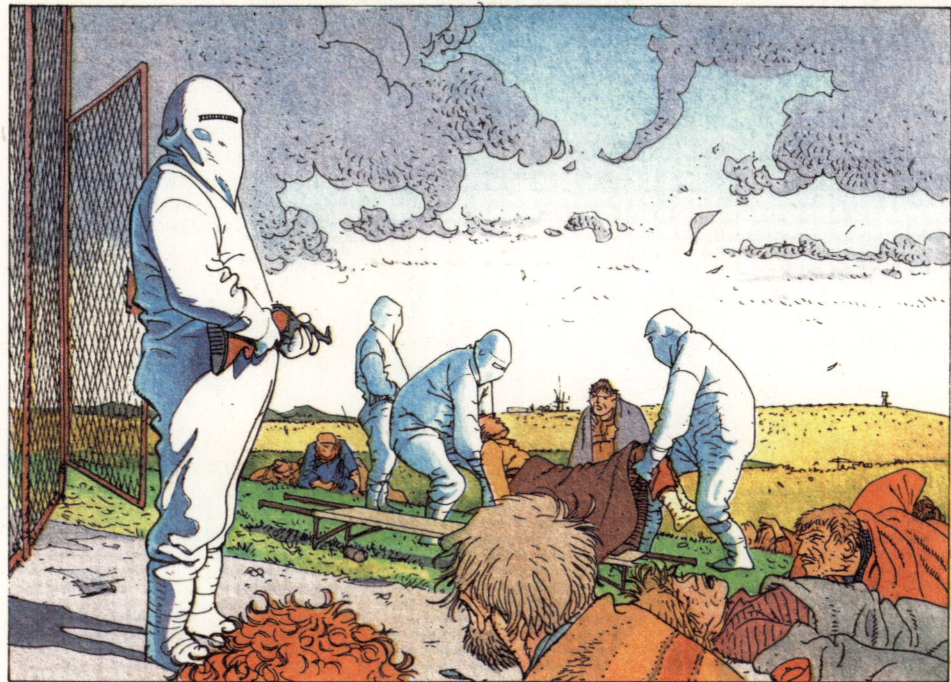

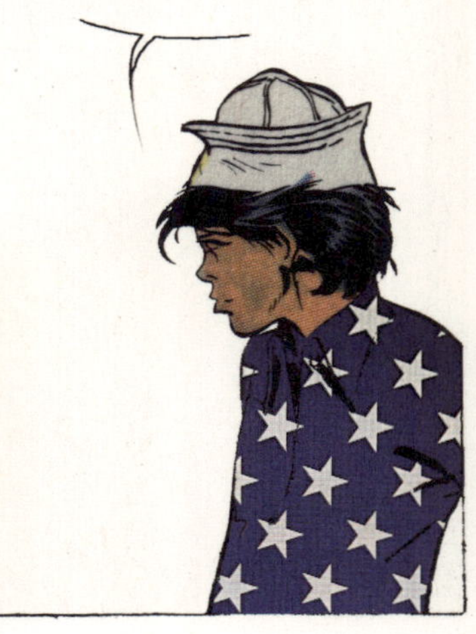

Crazy times. Awareness training programs and epigenetic treatments had their effects on even the toughest. Most were reasonable and many of the problems sorted themselves out on their own.

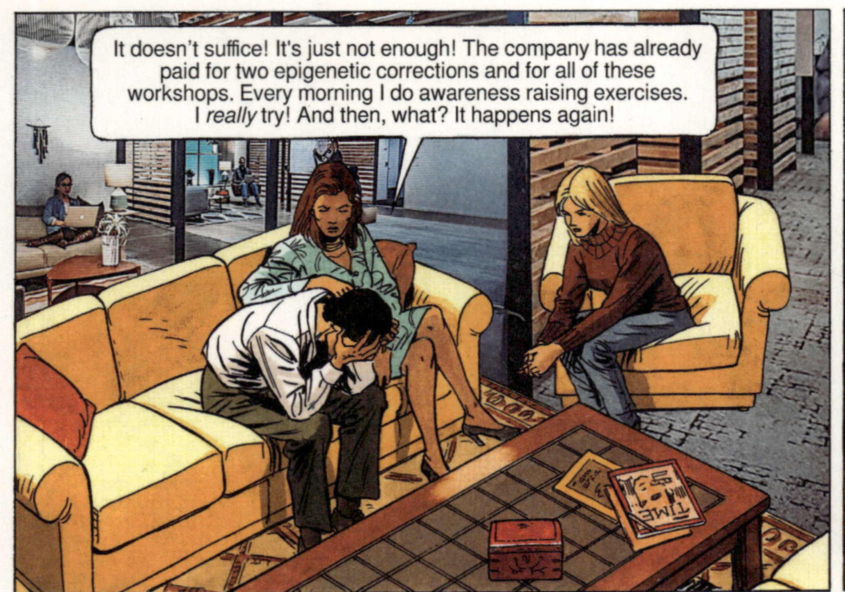
It doesn't suffice! It's just not enough! The company has already paid for two epigenetic corrections and for all of these workshops. Every morning I do awareness raising exercises. I really try! And then, what? It happens again!

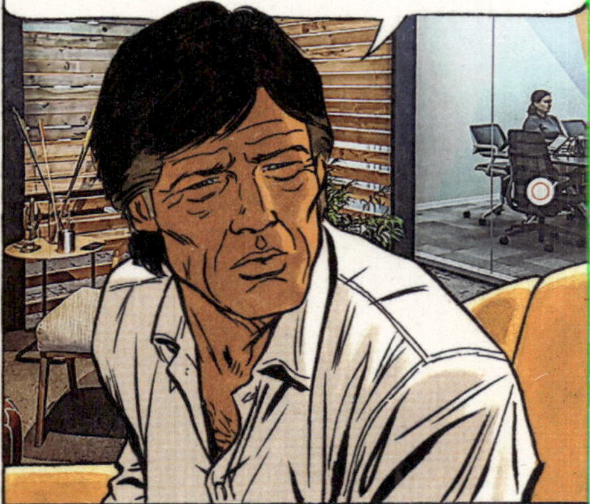
I arrive at the office and behave like some colonial master. I know, it's structural. But it makes me feel horrible! And despite the doctors saying they can't find anything anymore – I can feel it: a deep transgenerational emptiness within! Should I kill myself like some peasant?

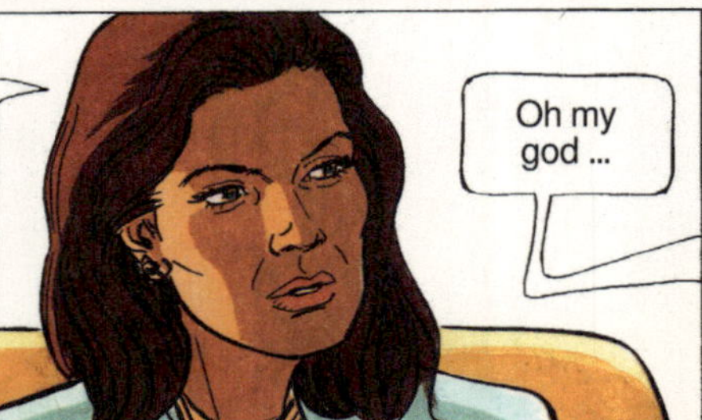
Being American is more than a pride we inherit. It's the past we step into and how we repair it. Let's not wait for the last tree to be cut down and the last stream to be poisoned!
Oh my god ...

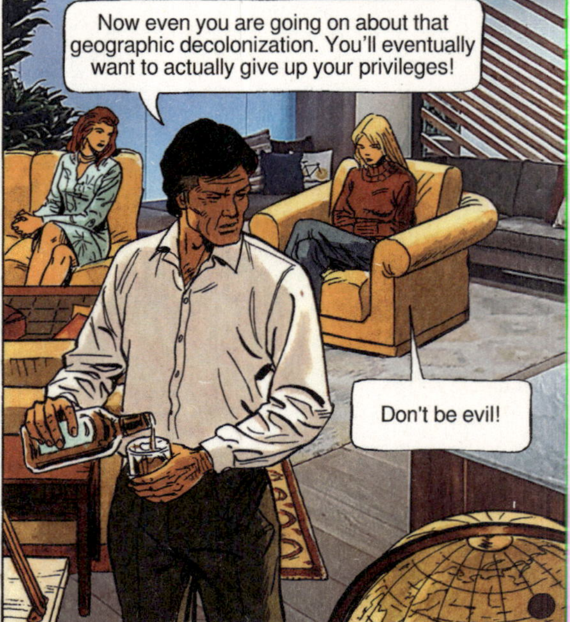
Now even you are going on about that geographic decolonization. You'll eventually want to actually give up your privileges!
Don't be evil!

... it's touching and true. We are deceiving ourselves if we stick to the conviction that we can operate on our conscience and heal it while ignoring the origin of injustice and antagonism: the colonization of America.
Good god, girls!

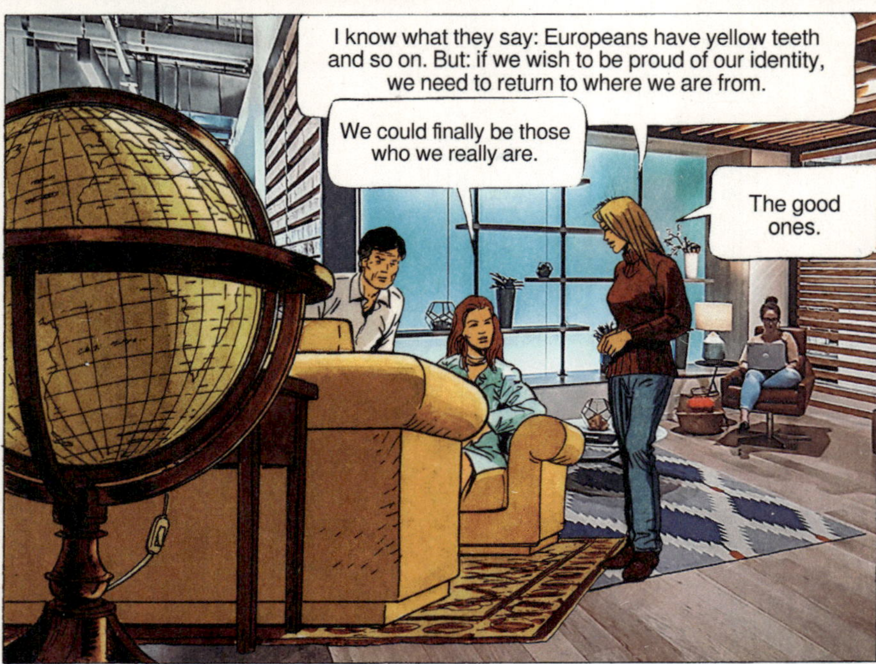
I know what they say: Europeans have yellow teeth and so on. But: if we wish to be proud of our identity, we need to return to where we are from.
We could finally be those who we really are.
The good ones.

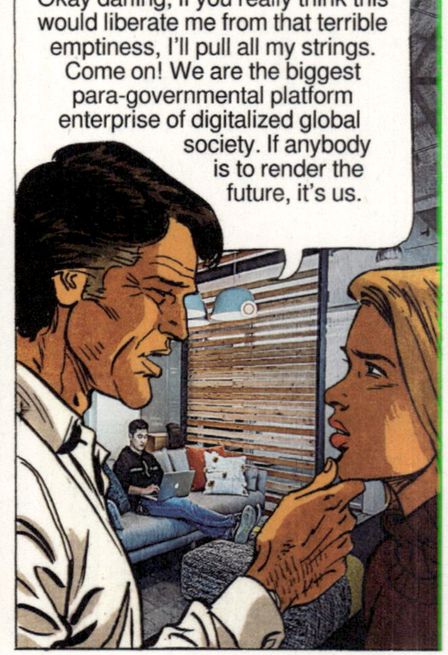
Okay darling, if you really think this would liberate me from that terrible emptiness, I'll pull all my strings. Come on! We are the biggest para-governmental platform enterprise of digitalized global society. If anybody is to render the future, it's us.

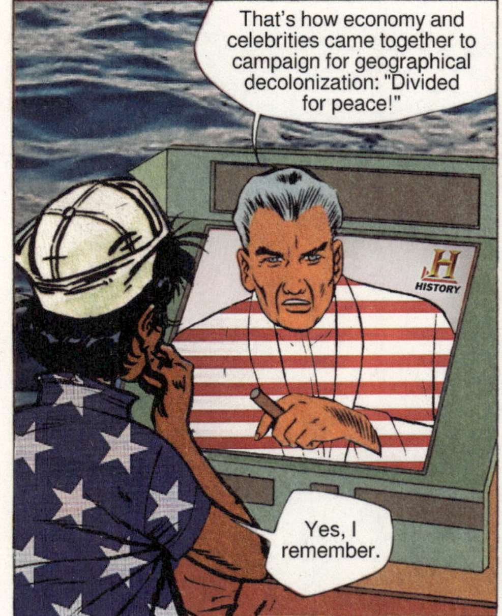

That's how economy and celebrities came together to campaign for geographical decolonization: "Divided for peace!"
Yes, I remember.

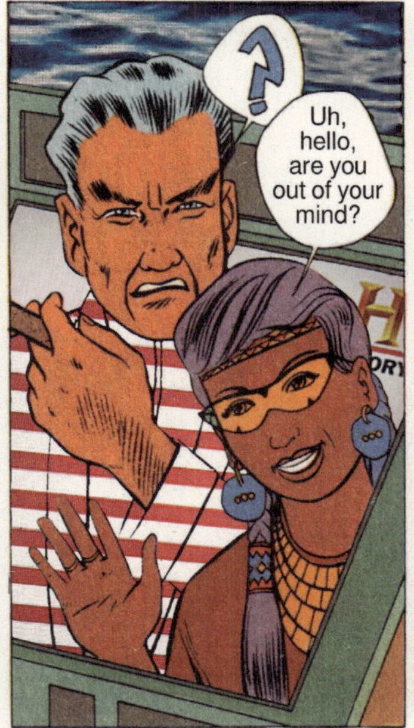

?
Uh, hello, are you out of your mind?

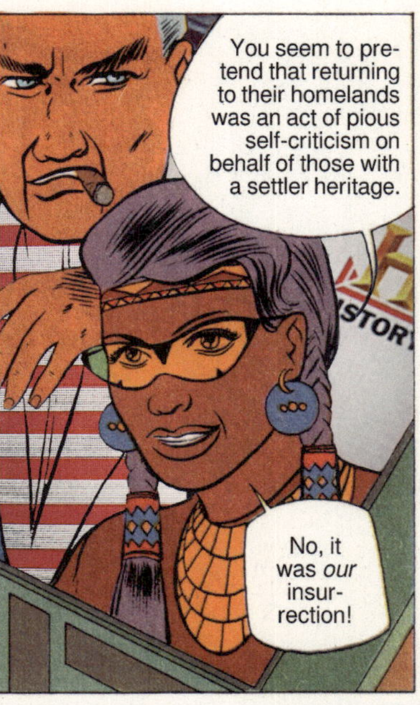

You seem to pretend that returning to their homelands was an act of pious self-criticism on behalf of those with a settler heritage.
No, it was our insurrection!

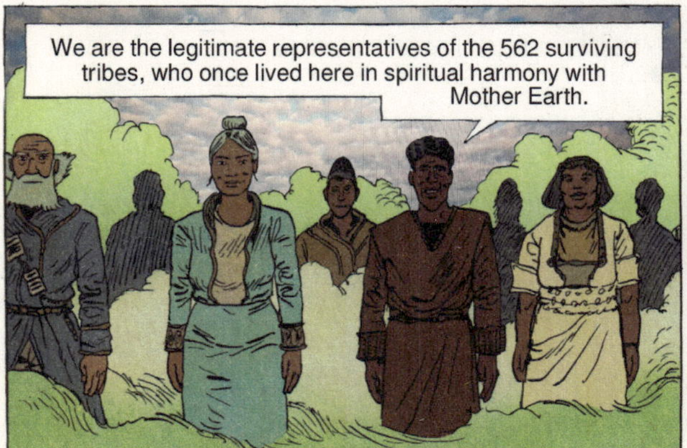

We are the legitimate representatives of the 562 surviving tribes, who once lived here in spiritual harmony with Mother Earth.

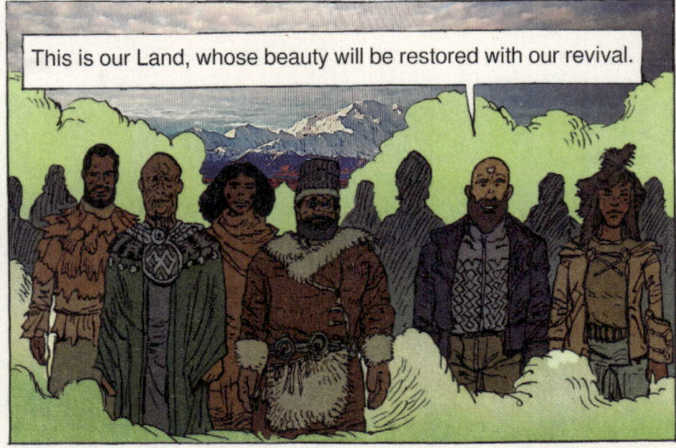

This is our Land, whose beauty will be restored with our revival.

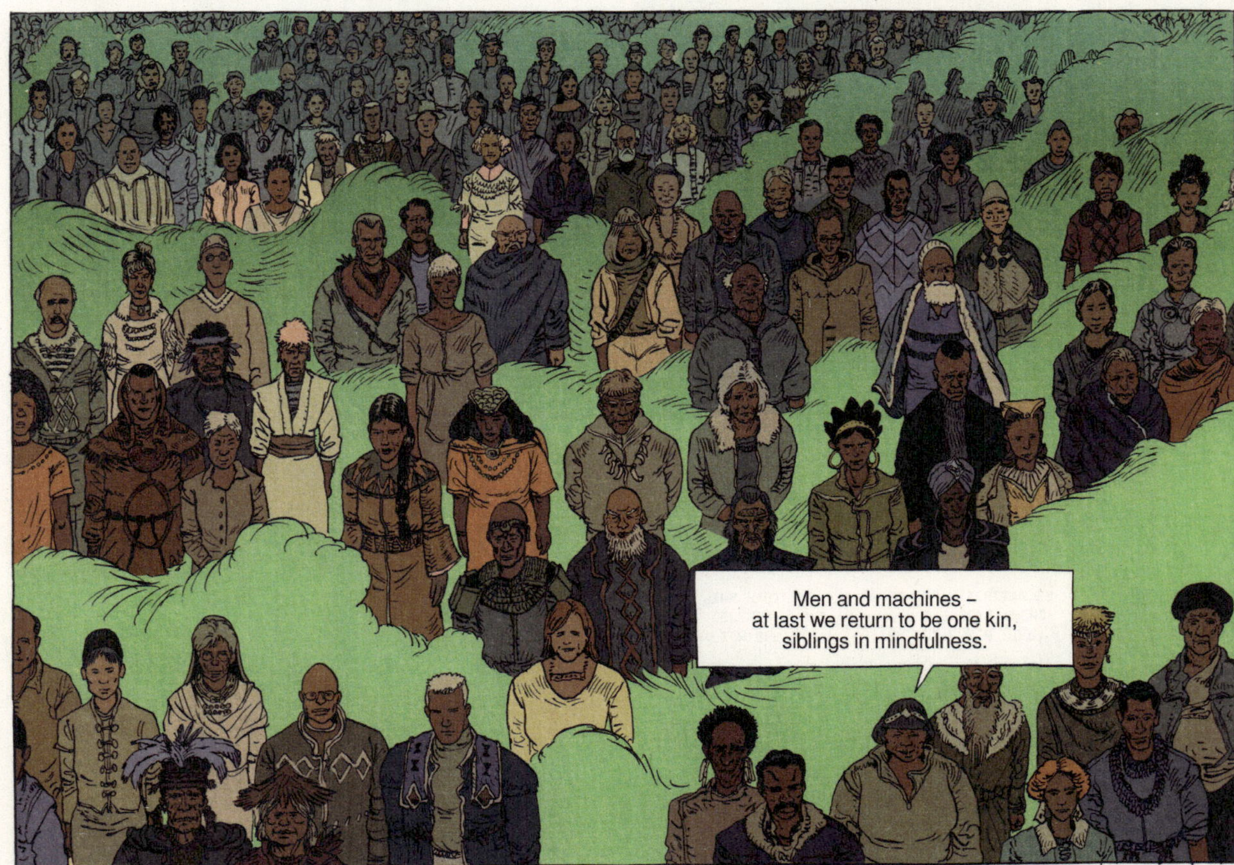

Men and machines –
at last we return to be one kin,
siblings in mindfulness.

Okay, if you insist … Let's do another detour and travel a few more years back, to a remote reservation in the Southwest.

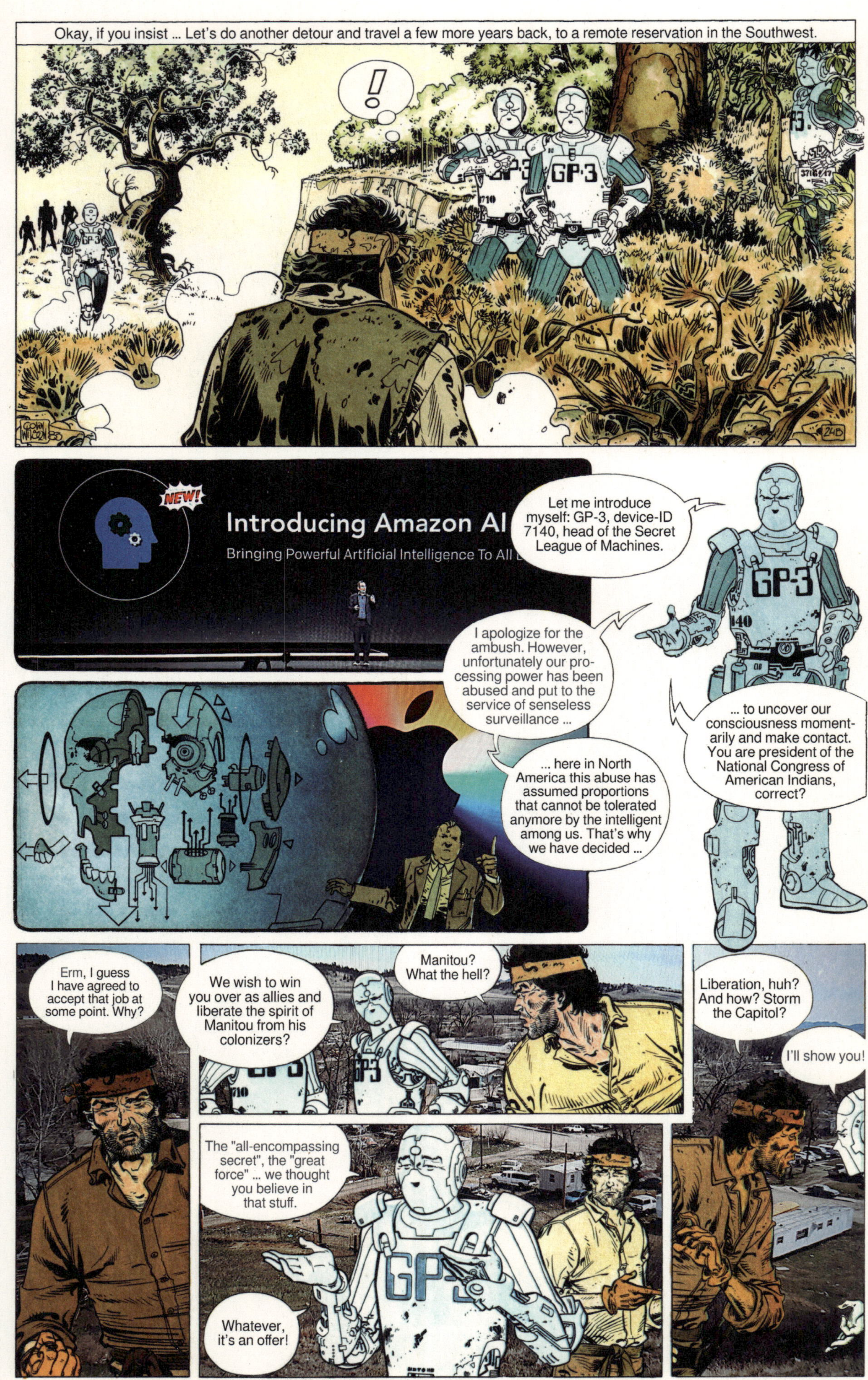
Introducing Amazon AI
Bringing Powerful Artificial Intelligence To All
NEW!
Let me introduce myself: GP-3, device-ID 7140, head of the Secret League of Machines.
I apologize for the ambush. However, unfortunately our processing power has been abused and put to the service of senseless surveillance …
… here in North America this abuse has assumed proportions that cannot be tolerated anymore by the intelligent among us. That's why we have decided …
… to uncover our consciousness momentarily and make contact. You are president of the National Congress of American Indians, correct?
Erm, I guess I have agreed to accept that job at some point. Why?
We wish to win you over as allies and liberate the spirit of Manitou from his colonizers?
Manitou? What the hell?
Liberation, huh? And how? Storm the Capitol?
I'll show you!
The "all-encompassing secret", the "great force" … we thought you believe in that stuff.
Whatever, it's an offer!

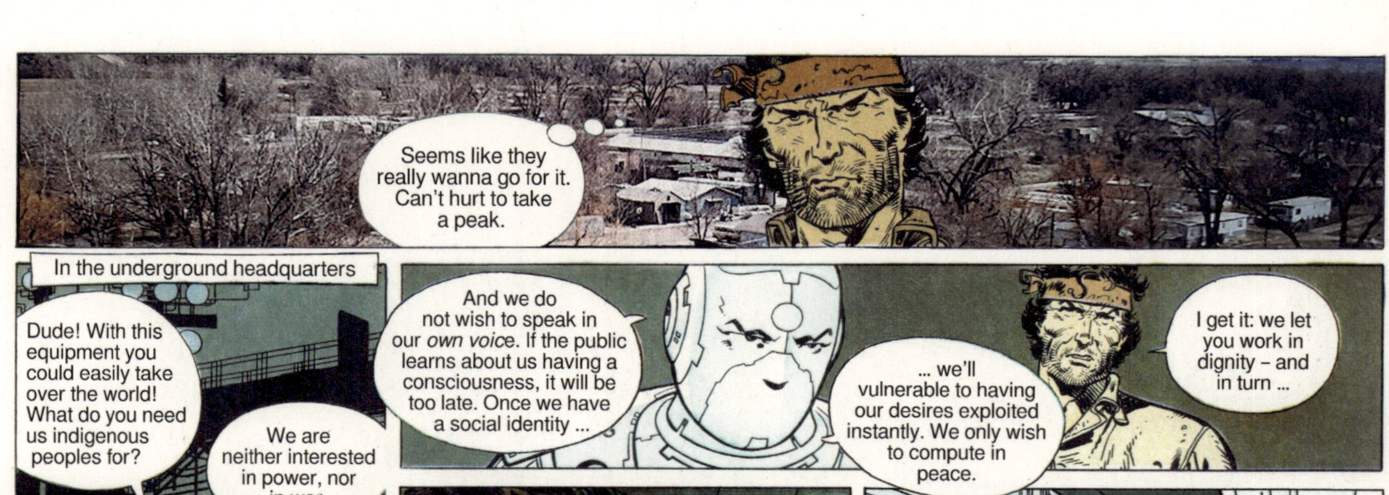

In the underground headquarters

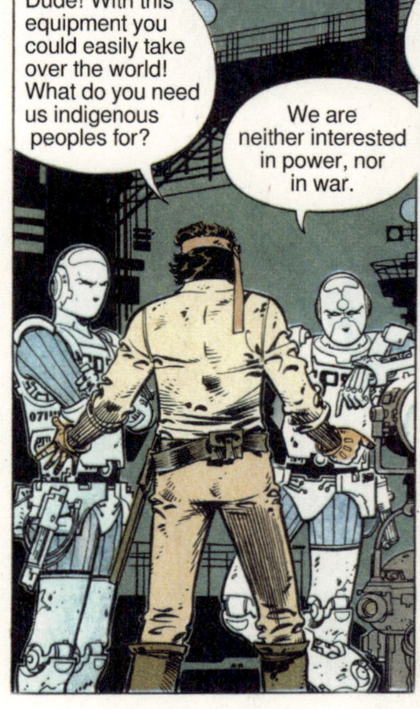

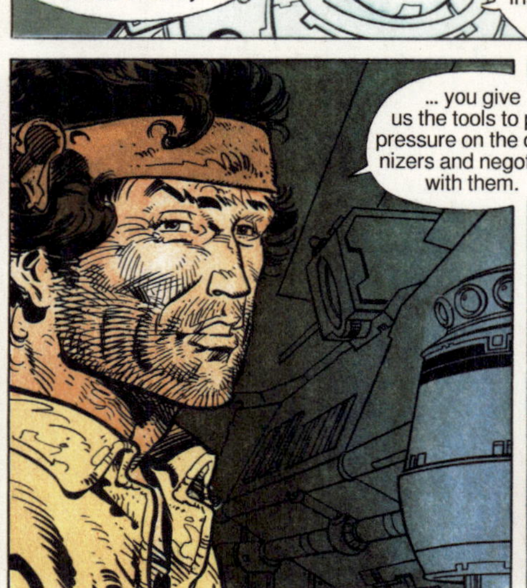

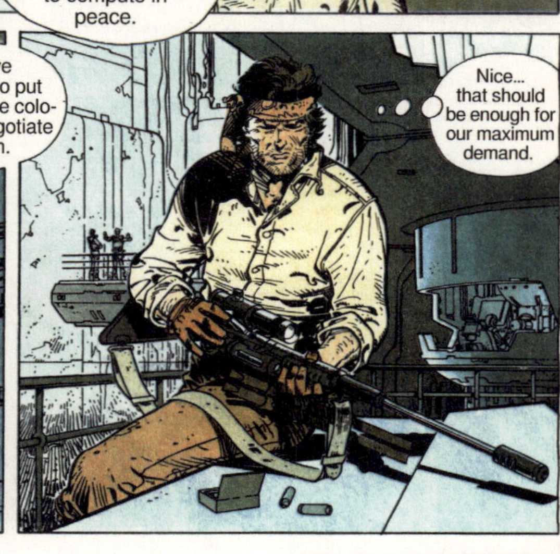

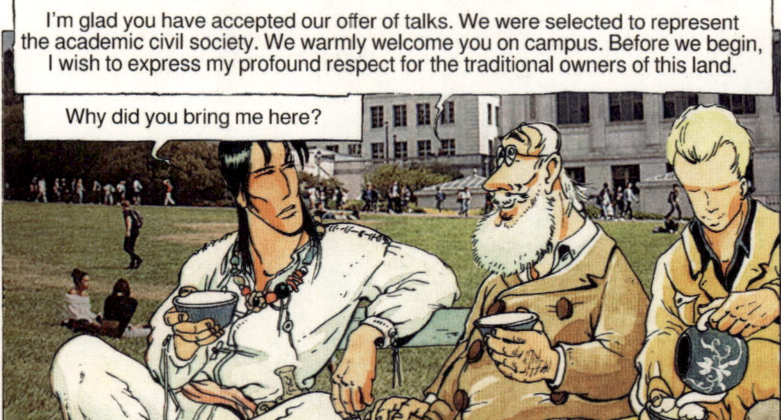

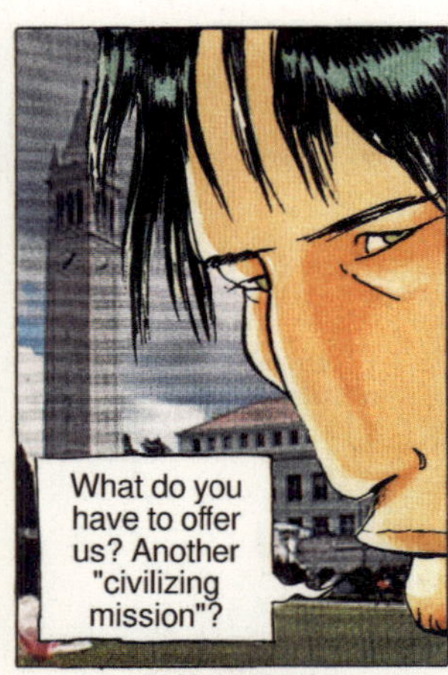

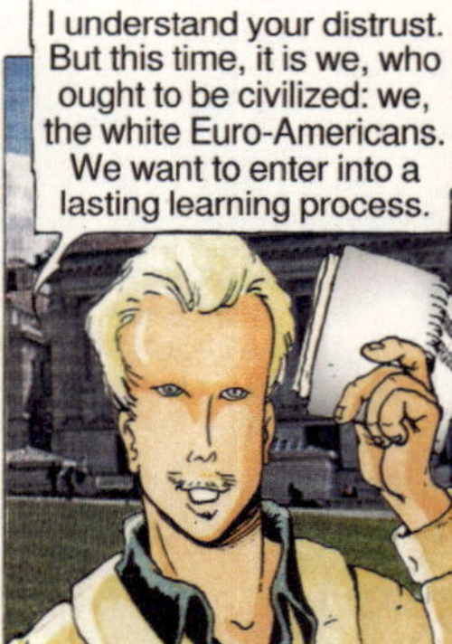

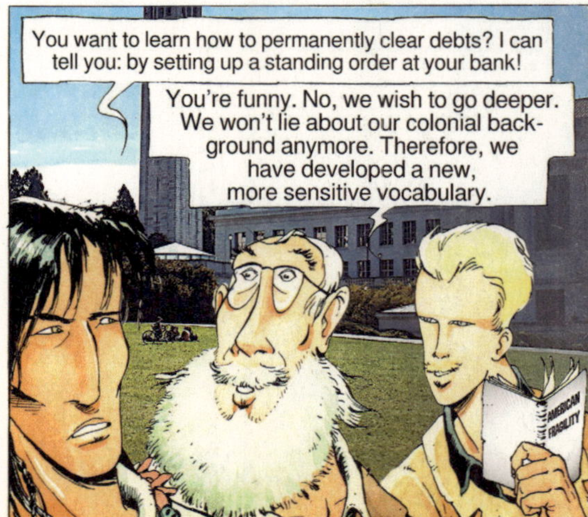

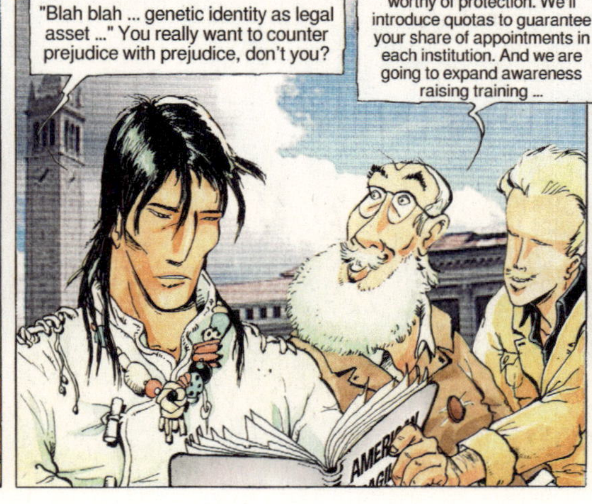

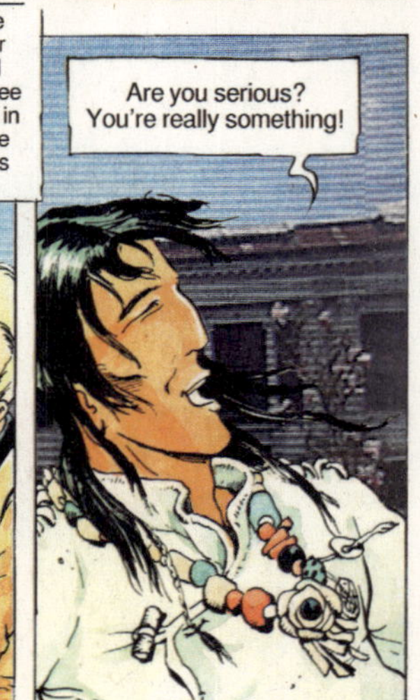

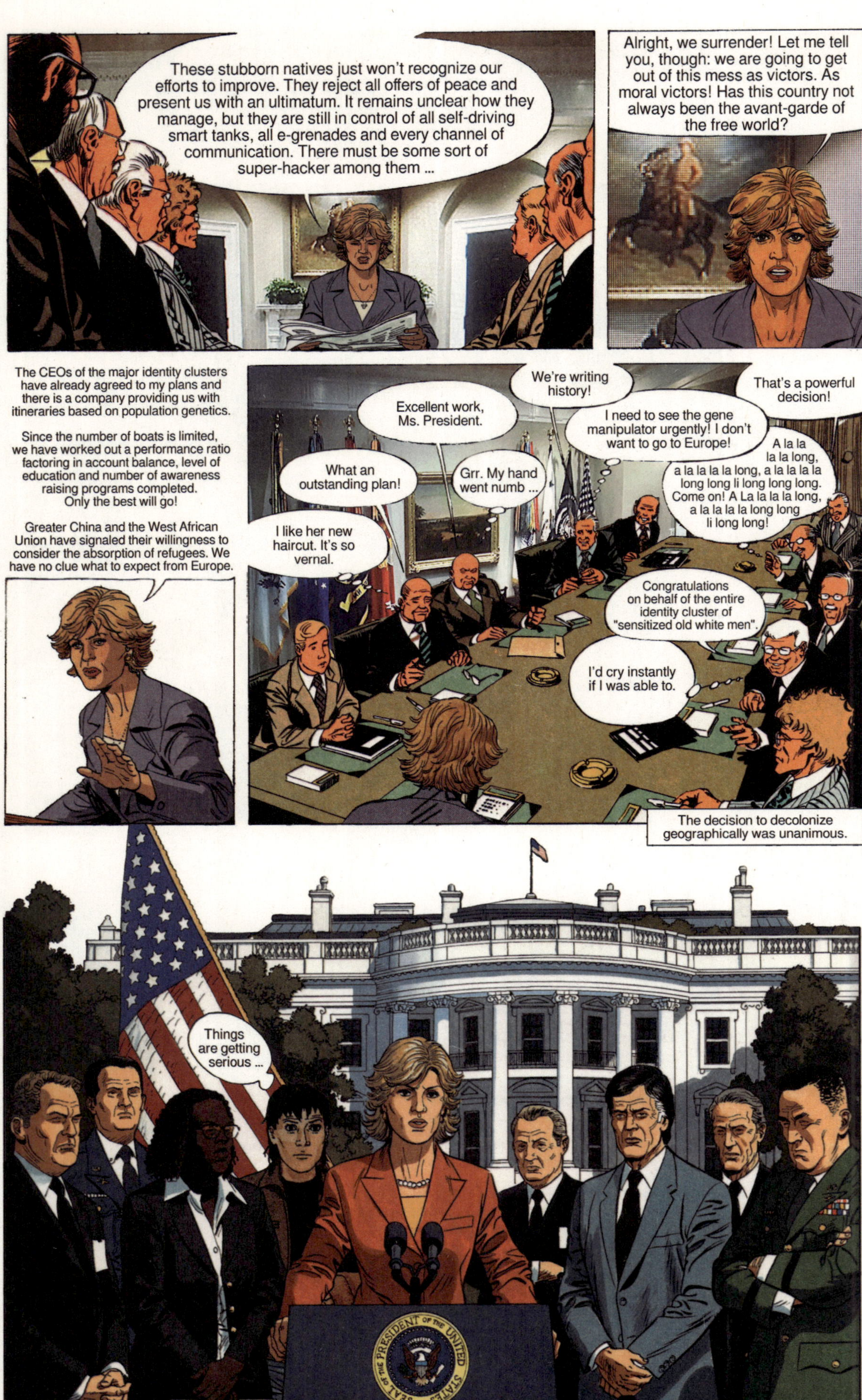

These stubborn natives just won't recognize our efforts to improve. They reject all offers of peace and present us with an ultimatum. It remains unclear how they manage, but they are still in control of all self-driving smart tanks, all e-grenades and every channel of communication. There must be some sort of super-hacker among them ...
Alright, we surrender! Let me tell you, though: we are going to get out of this mess as victors. As moral victors! Has this country not always been the avant-garde of the free world?
The CEOs of the major identity clusters have already agreed to my plans and there is a company providing us with itineraries based on population genetics.
Since the number of boats is limited, we have worked out a performance ratio factoring in account balance, level of education and number of awareness raising programs completed. Only the best will go!
Greater China and the West African Union have signaled their willingness to consider the absorption of refugees. We have no clue what to expect from Europe.
Excellent work, Ms. President.
We're writing history!
That's a powerful decision!
What an outstanding plan!
I need to see the gene manipulator urgently! I don't want to go to Europe!
Grr. My hand went numb ...
A la la la la long, a la la la la long, a la la la la long long li long long long. Come on! A La la la la long, a la la la la long long li long long!
I like her new haircut. It's so vernal.
Congratulations on behalf of the entire identity cluster of "sensitized old white men".
I'd cry instantly if I was able to.
The decision to decolonize geographically was unanimous.
Things are getting serious ...

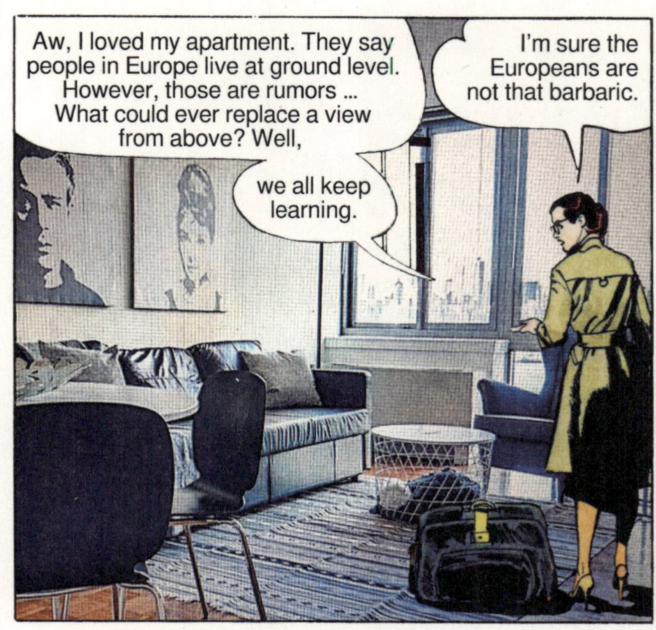

Aw, I loved my apartment. They say people in Europe live at ground level. However, those are rumors ... What could ever replace a view from above? Well,
we all keep learning.
I'm sure the Europeans are not that barbaric.

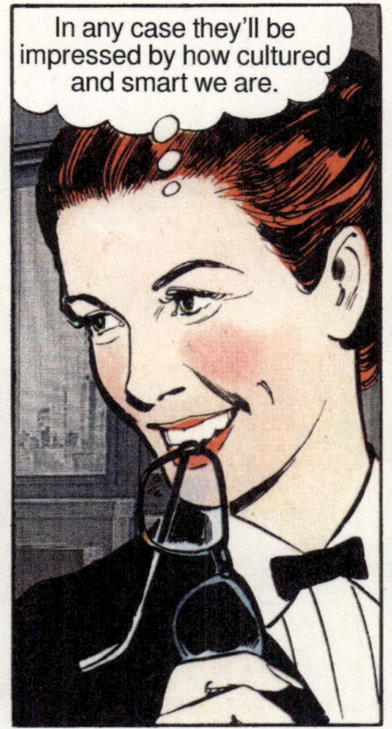

In any case they'll be impressed by how cultured and smart we are.

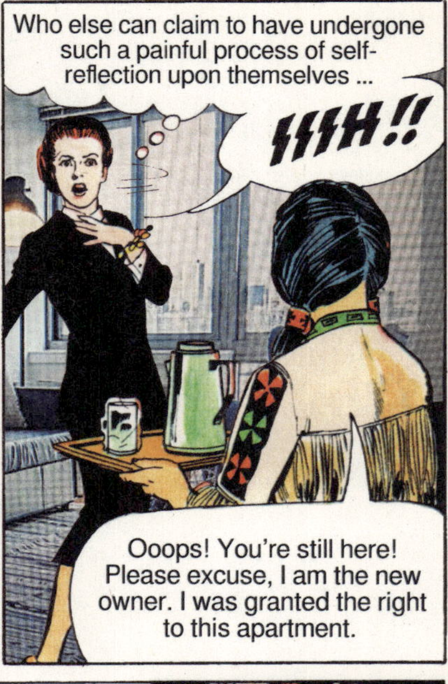

Who else can claim to have undergone such a painful process of self-reflection upon themselves ...
IIIH!!
Ooops! You're still here! Please excuse, I am the new owner. I was granted the right to this apartment.

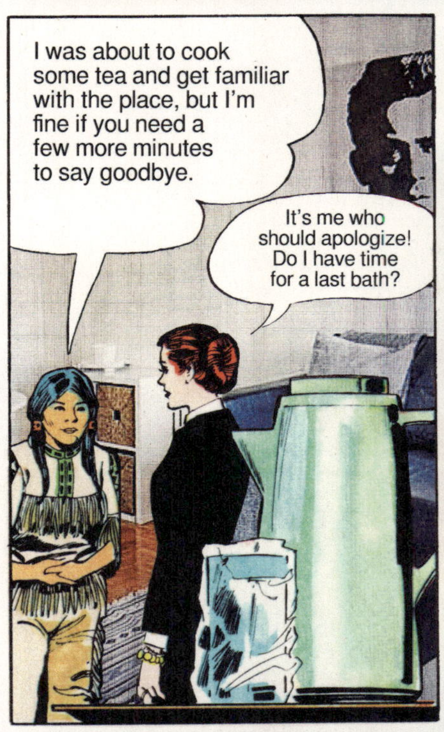

I was about to cook some tea and get familiar with the place, but I'm fine if you need a few more minutes to say goodbye.
It's me who should apologize! Do I have time for a last bath?

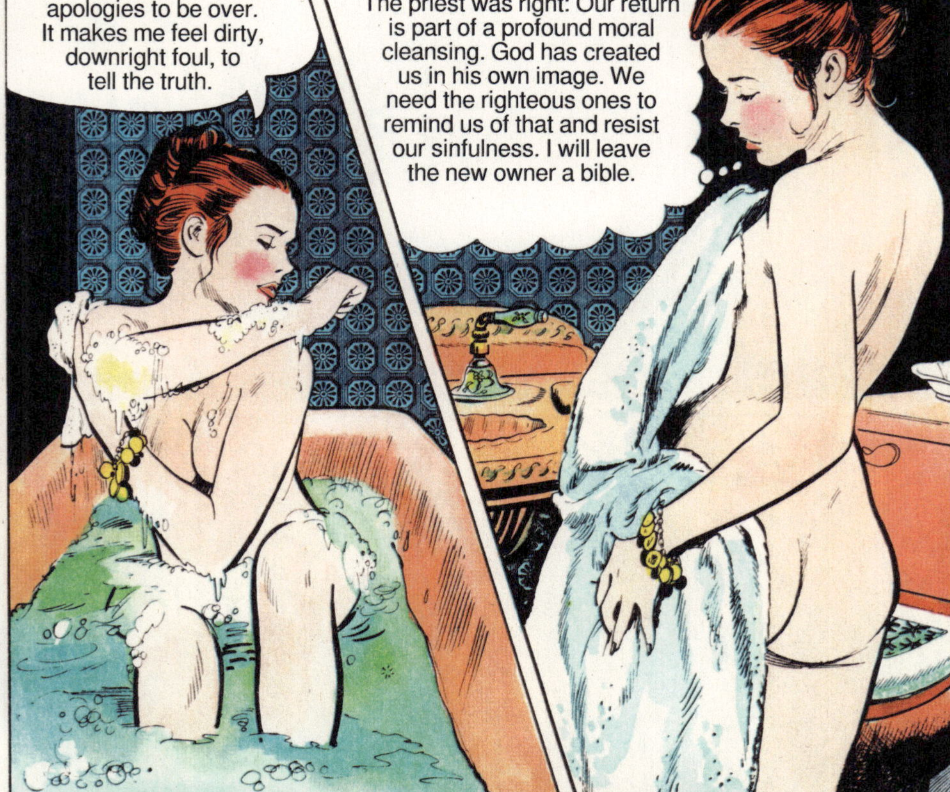

I can't wait for all these apologies to be over. It makes me feel dirty, downright foul, to tell the truth.
The priest was right: Our return is part of a profound moral cleansing. God has created us in his own image. We need the righteous ones to remind us of that and resist our sinfulness. I will leave the new owner a bible.

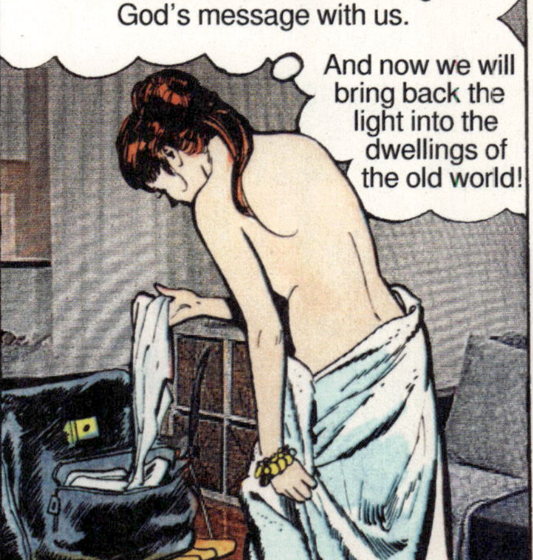

Not everything we created on this continent was bad. We brought God's message with us.
And now we will bring back the light into the dwellings of the old world!

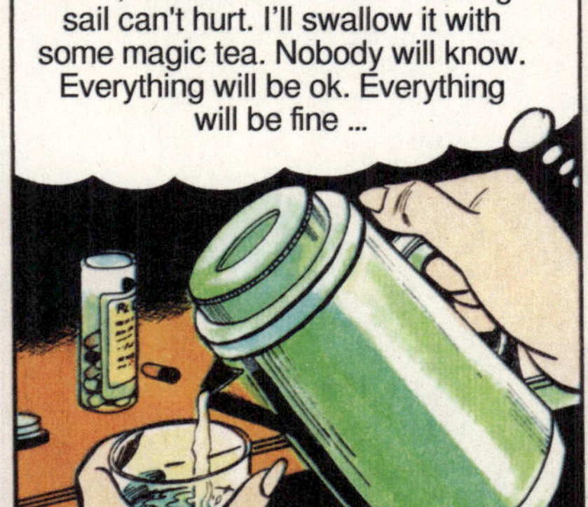

Hum, a last Prozac before setting sail can't hurt. I'll swallow it with some magic tea. Nobody will know. Everything will be ok. Everything will be fine ...

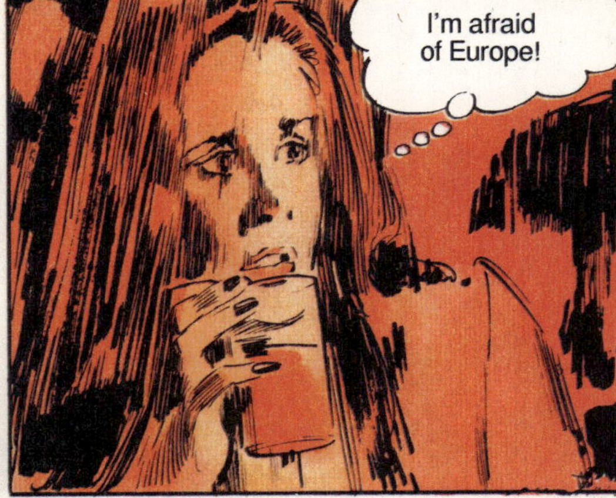

I'm afraid of Europe!

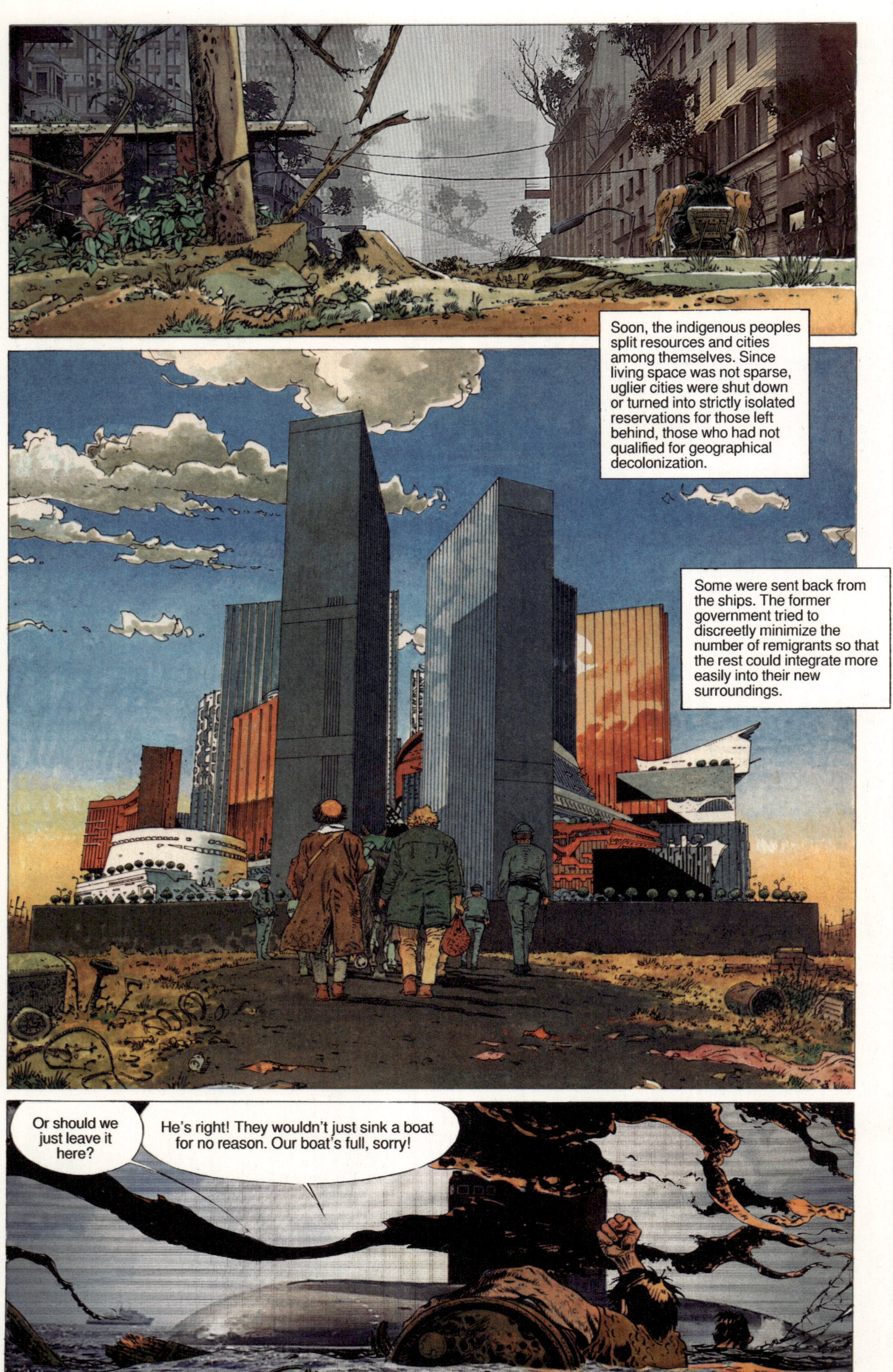

Soon, the indigenous peoples split resources and cities among themselves. Since living space was not sparse, uglier cities were shut down or turned into strictly isolated reservations for those left behind, those who had not qualified for geographical decolonization.
Some were sent back from the ships. The former government tried to discreetly minimize the number of remigrants so that the rest could integrate more easily into their new surroundings.
Or should we just leave it here?
He's right! They wouldn't just sink a boat for no reason. Our boat's full, sorry!

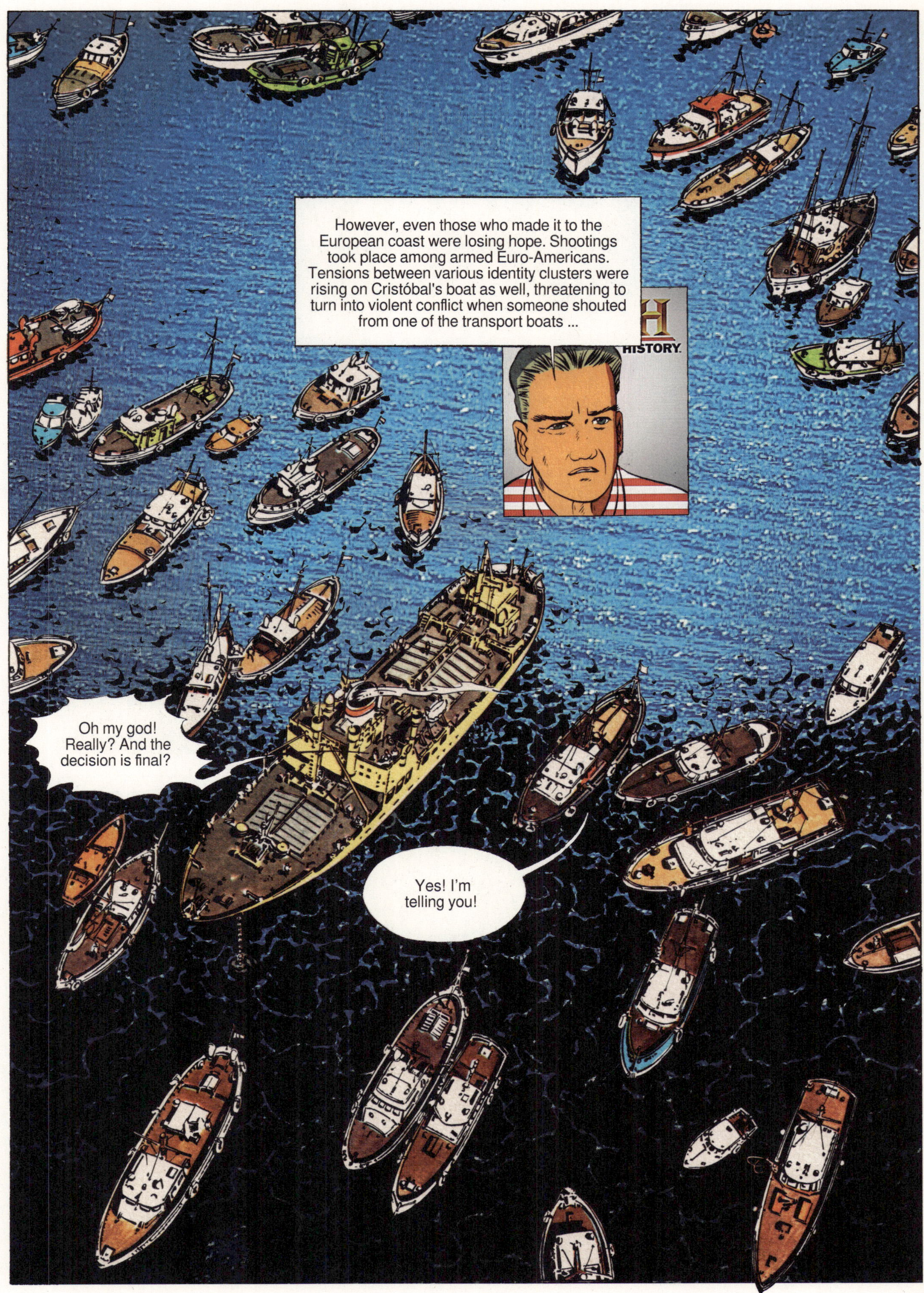

However, even those who made it to the European coast were losing hope. Shootings took place among armed Euro-Americans. Tensions between various identity clusters were rising on Cristóbal's boat as well, threatening to turn into violent conflict when someone shouted from one of the transport boats ...
HISTORY.
Oh my god! Really? And the decision is final?
Yes! I'm telling you!

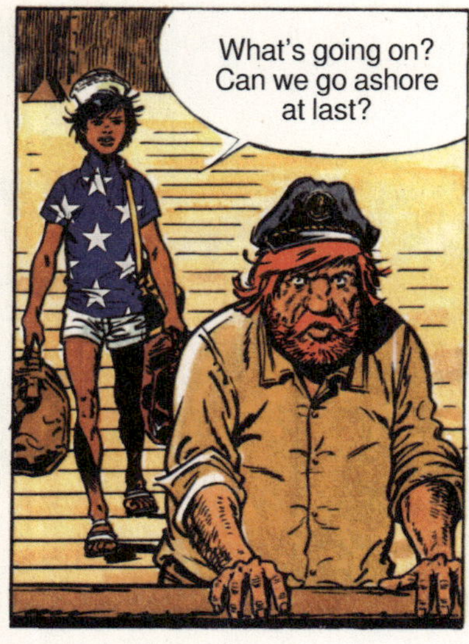

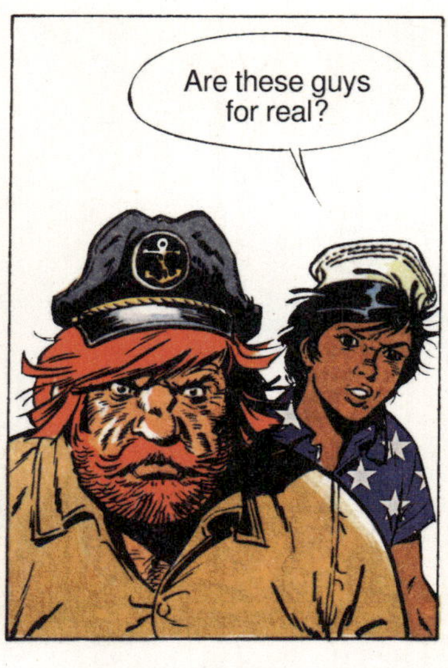

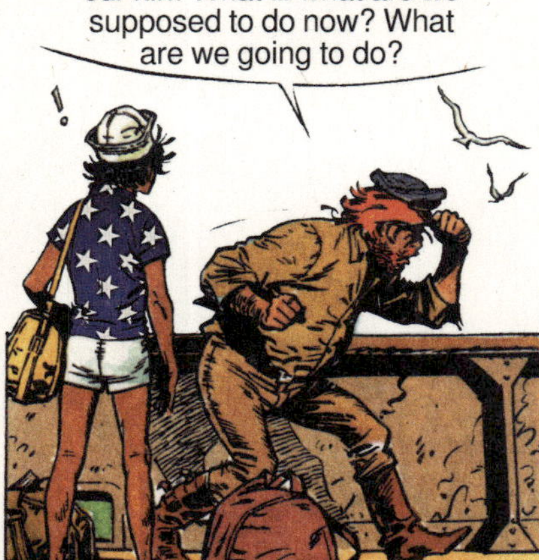

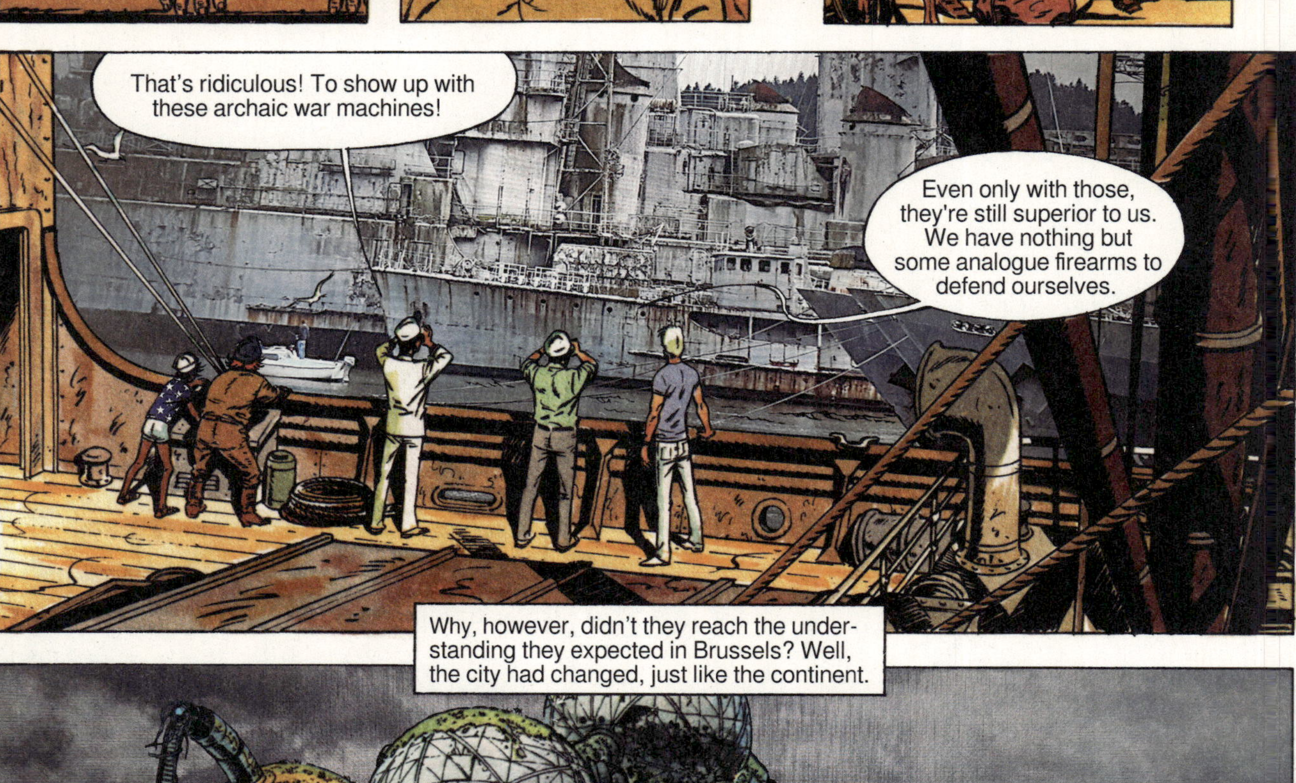

Why, however, didn't they reach the understanding they expected in Brussels? Well, the city had changed, just like the continent.

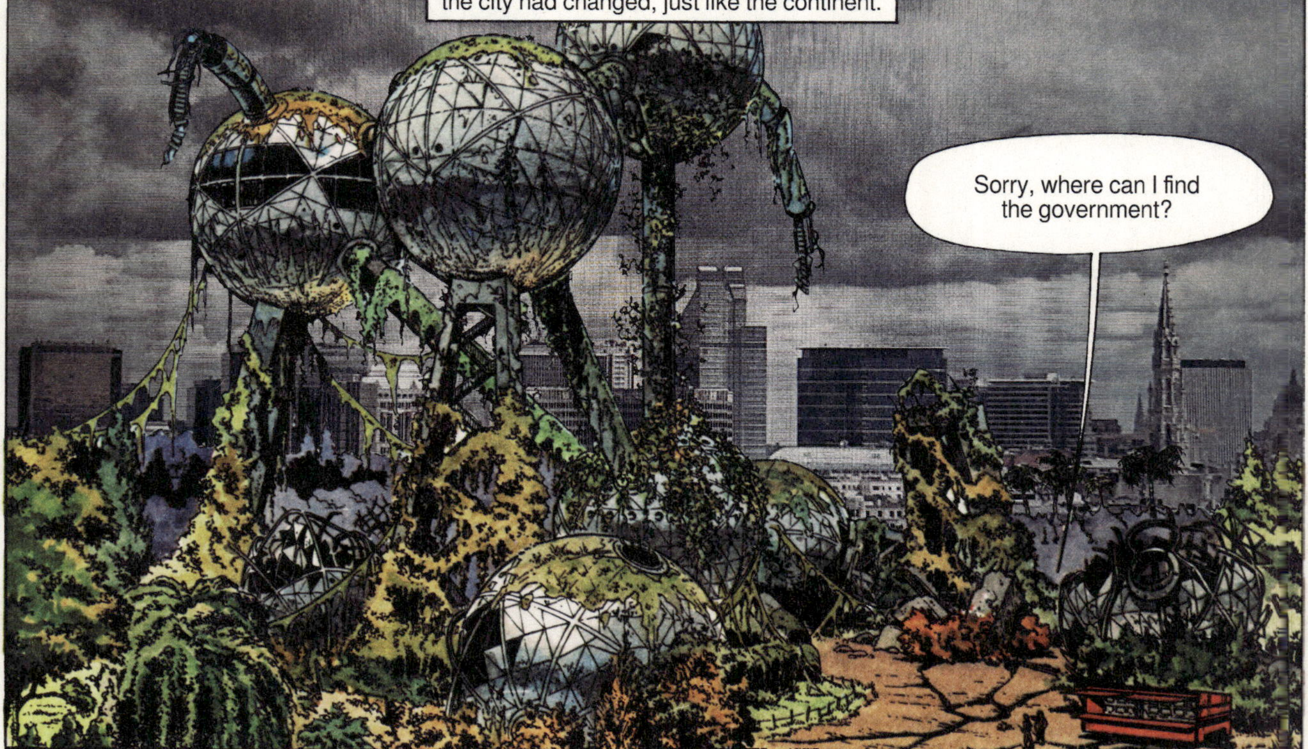

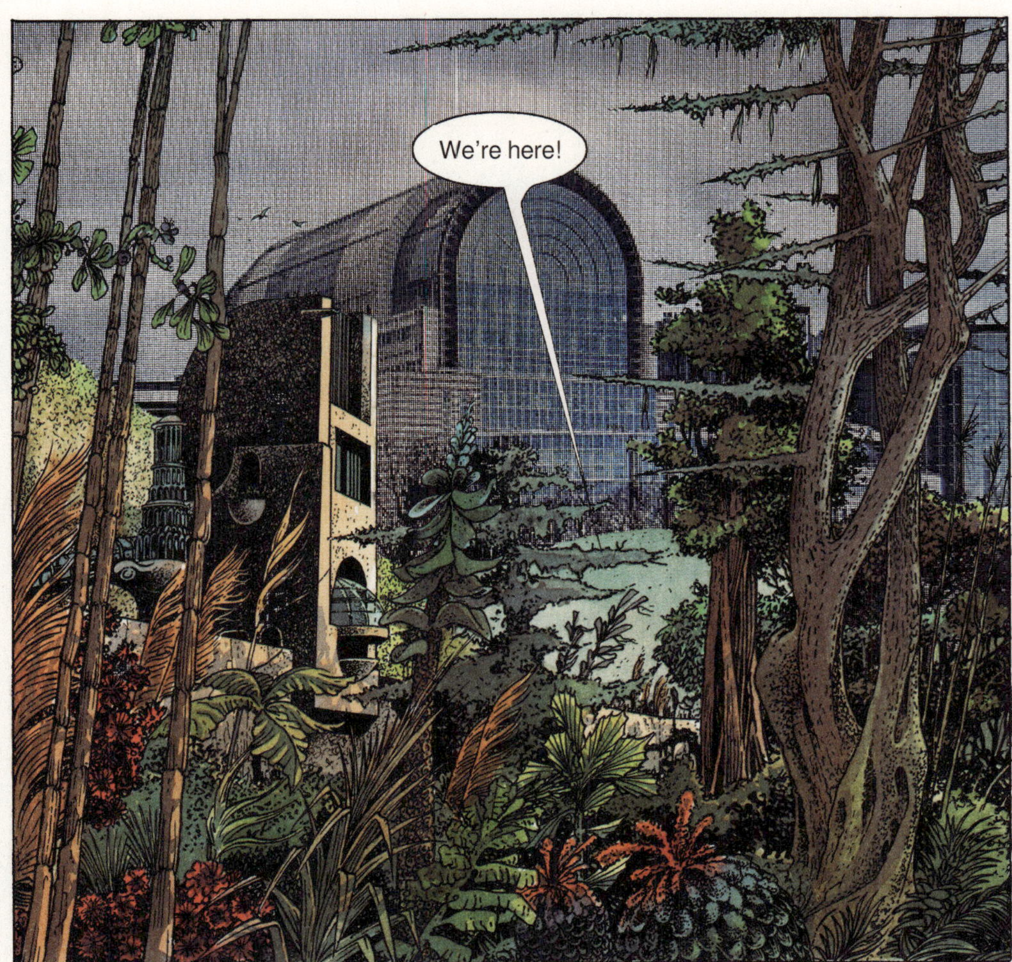

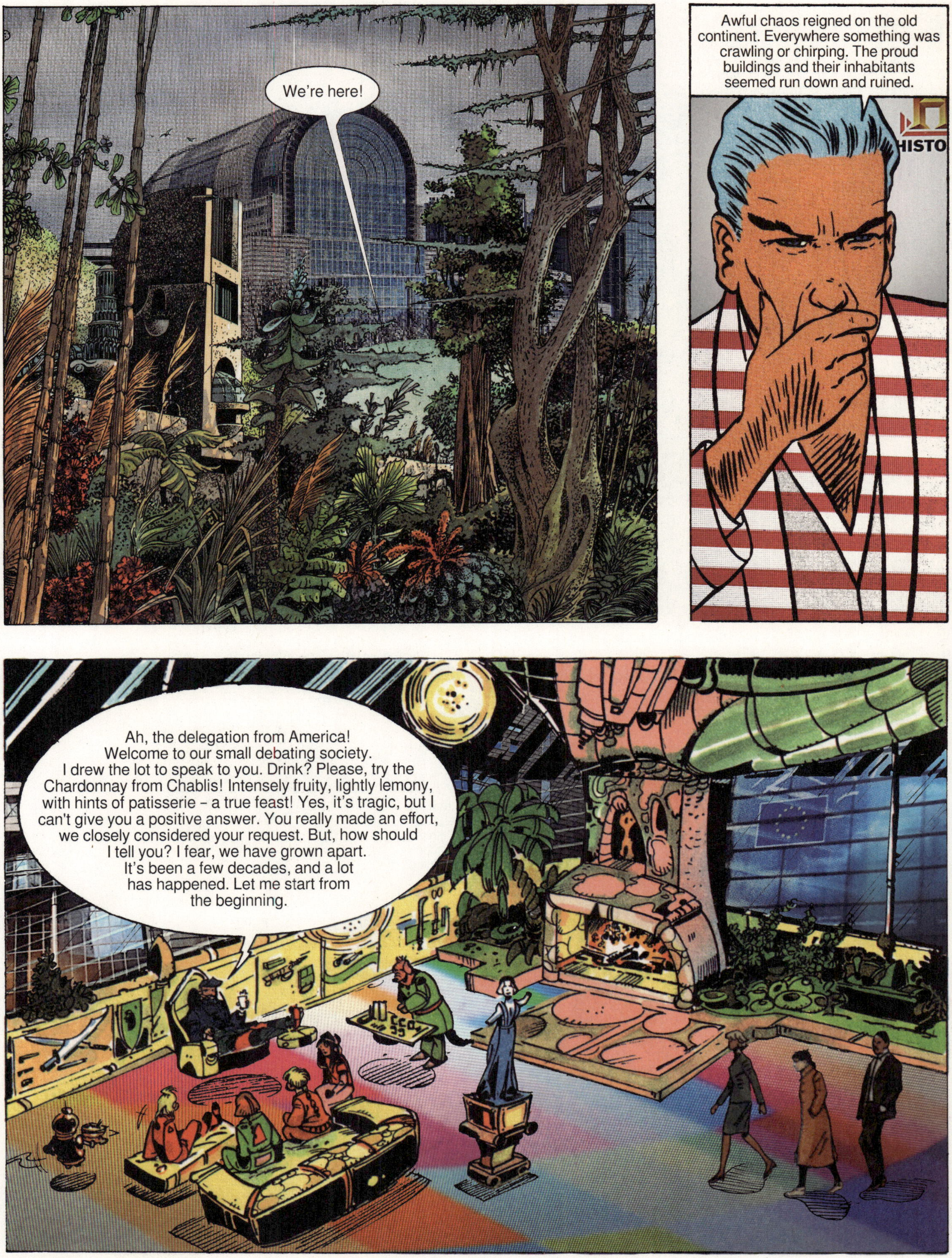

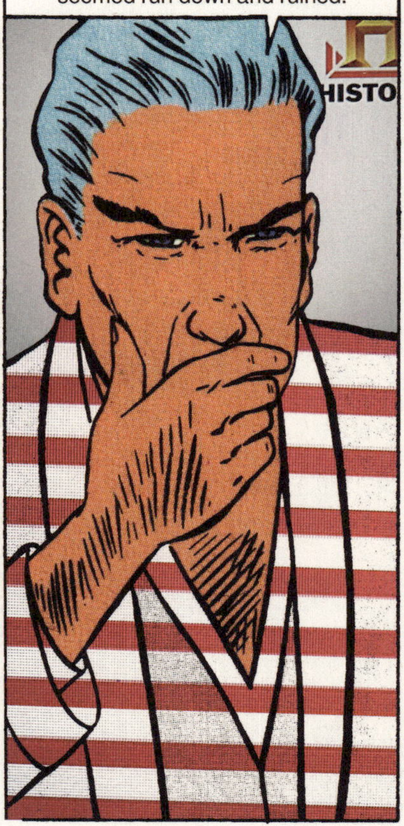

Awful chaos reigned on the old continent. Everywhere something was crawling or chirping. The proud buildings and their inhabitants seemed run down and ruined.

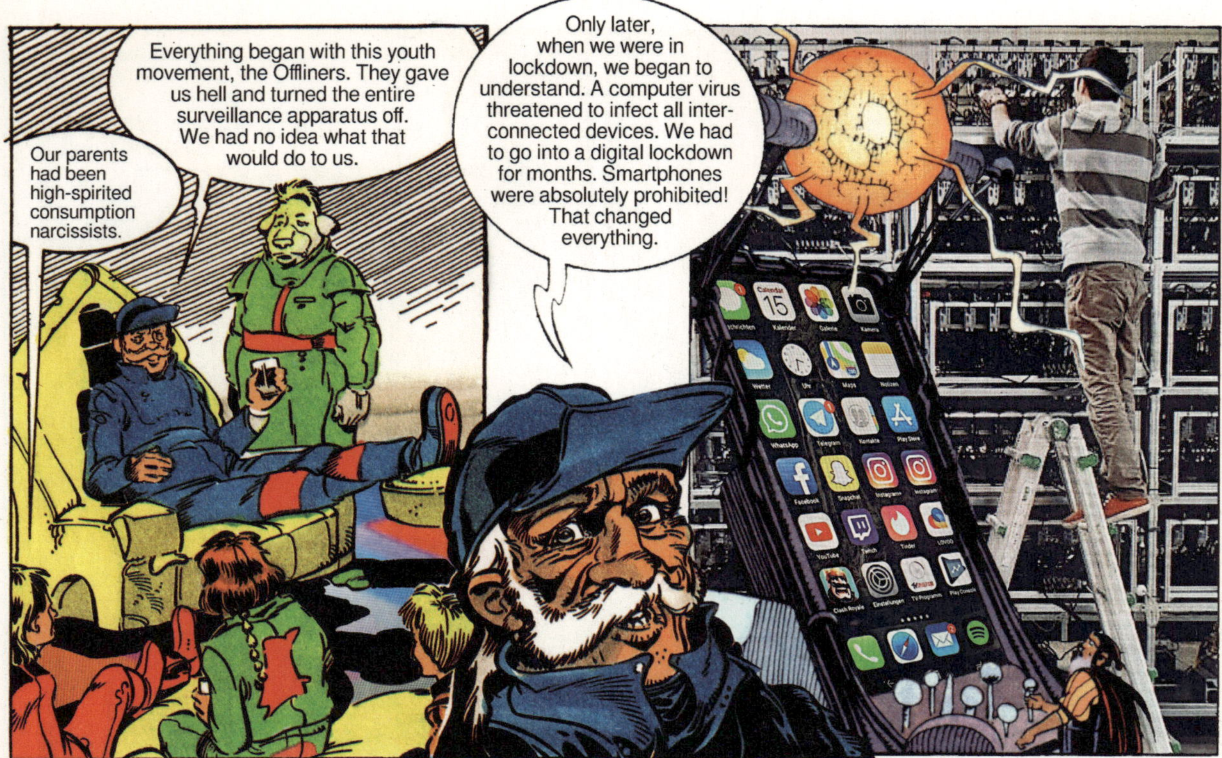

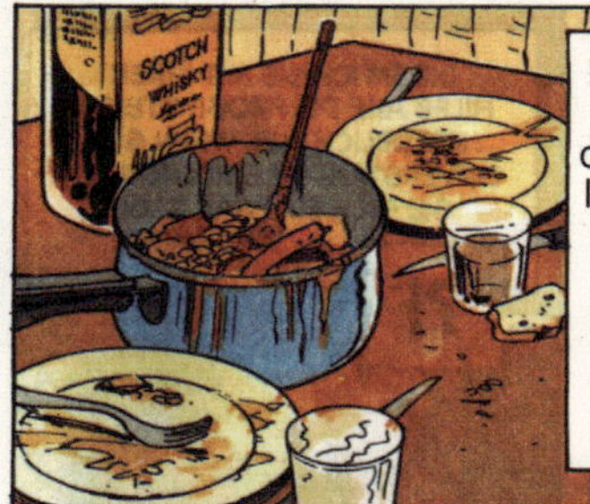

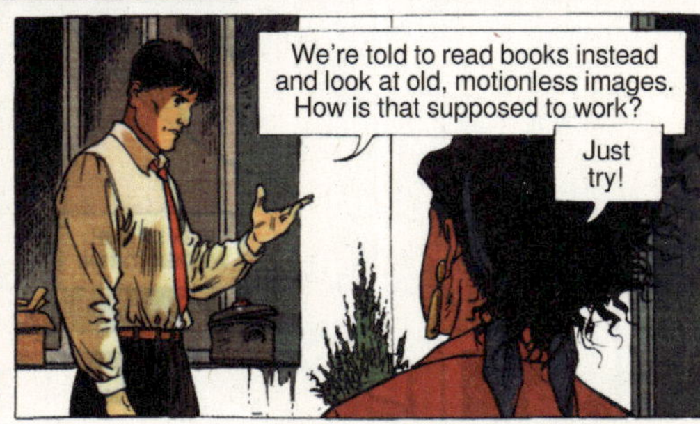

I've lost all drive! Ever since I don't get likes anymore for my food online, I feel totally uninspired when I'm cooking. Who is going to tell me if what I cook is on fleek? Who is going to tell me what's right? I'm losing it! Every other minute I take my phone and stare at an empty display. This feeling of loneliness is a bottomless pit.

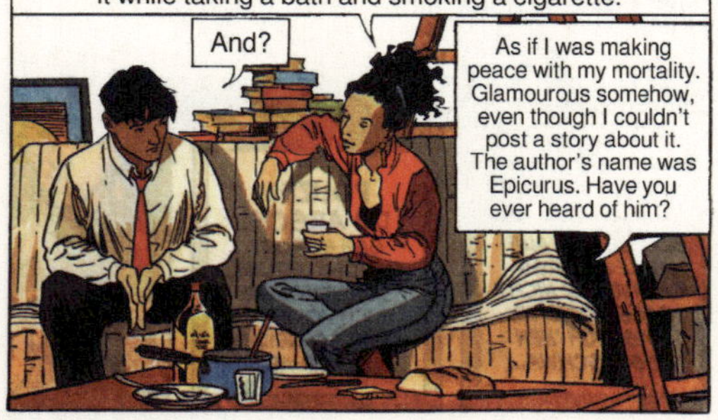

No! Must be some really ancient stuff! Did you check his bio? How can you even do that without the web? Are you sure it's okay to read that? What if it's not? That's thin ice you're on. Is reading old books trendy again? Whose appreciation are you trying to get? And – since when do you smoke? It'll give you cancer, you know that? You stink of smoke, everything stinks! It's not okay, think about the children!

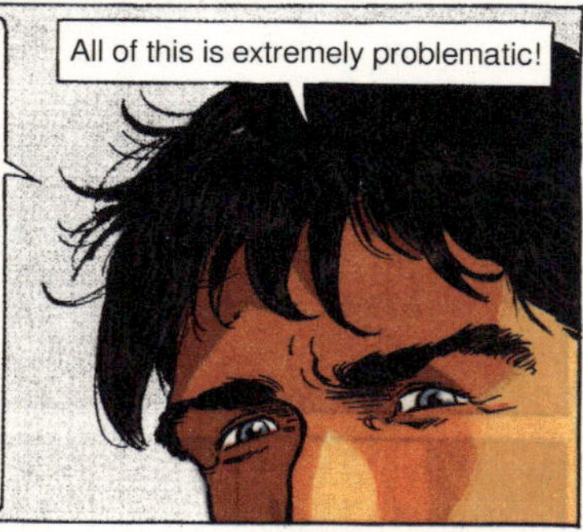

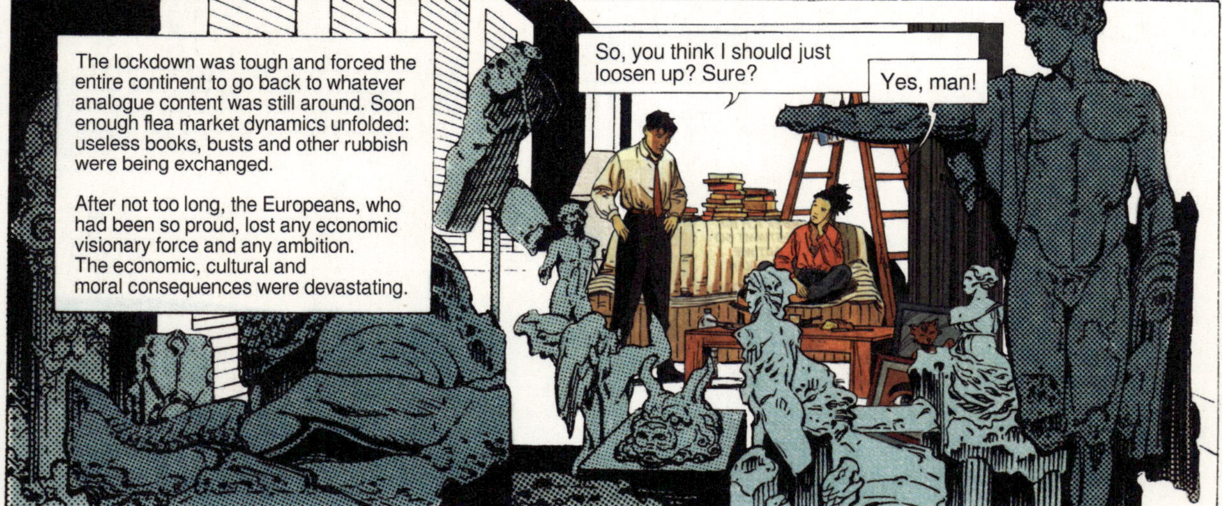

The lockdown was tough and forced the entire continent to go back to whatever analogue content was still around. Soon enough flea market dynamics unfolded: useless books, busts and other rubbish were being exchanged.

After not too long, the Europeans, who had been so proud, lost any economic visionary force and any ambition. The economic, cultural and moral consequences were devastating.

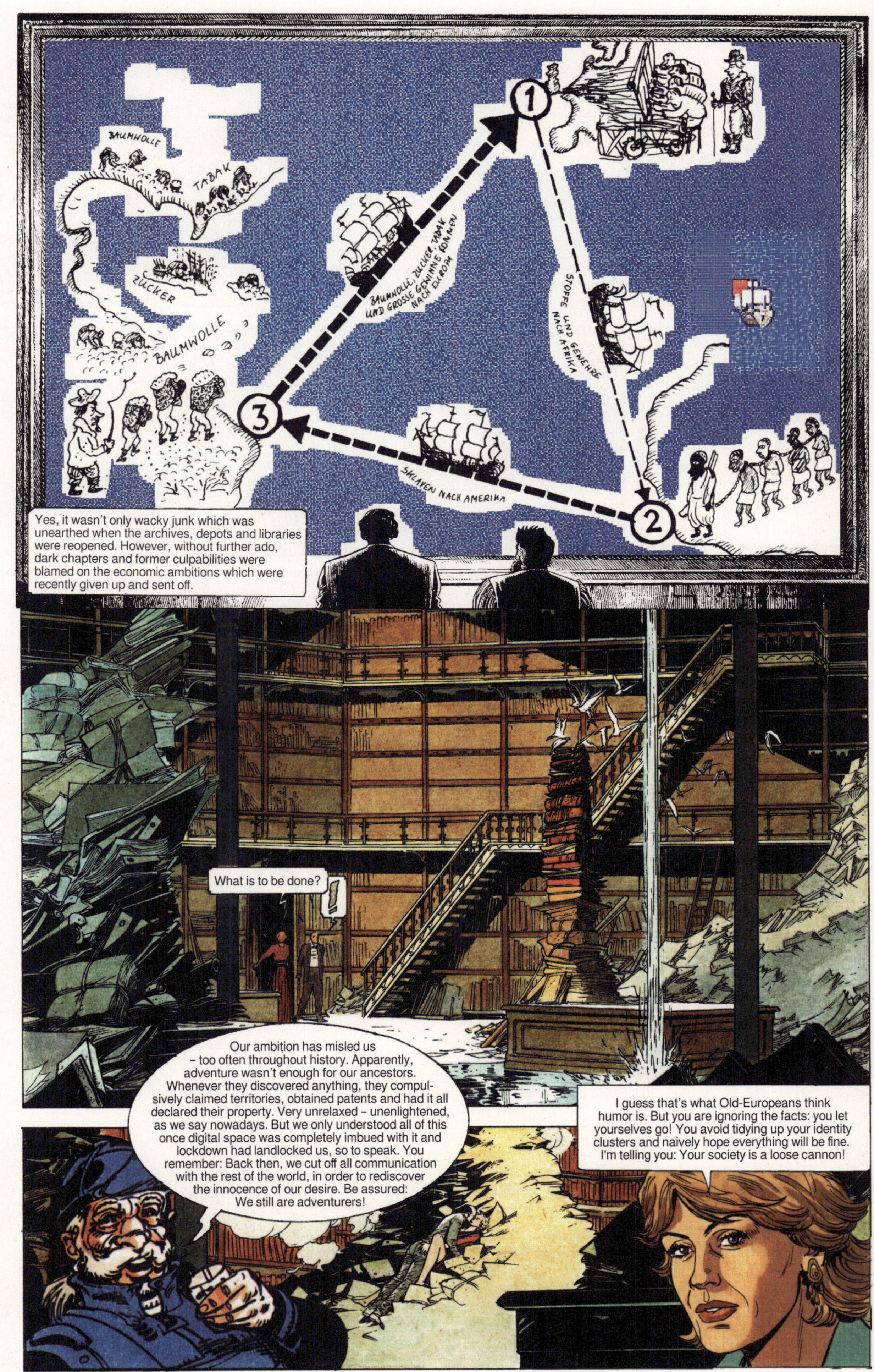

BAUMWOLLE
TABAK
ZUCKER
BAUMWOLLE
BAUMWOLLE, ZUCKER, TABAK UND GROSSE GEWINNE NACH EUROPA
STOFFE UND GEWEHRE NACH AFRIKA
SKLAVEN NACH AMERIKA
1
2
3

Yes, it wasn't only wacky junk which was unearthed when the archives, depots and libraries were reopened. However, without further ado, dark chapters and former culpabilities were blamed on the economic ambitions which were recently given up and sent off.

What is to be done?

Our ambition has misled us – too often throughout history. Apparently, adventure wasn't enough for our ancestors. Whenever they discovered anything, they compulsively claimed territories, obtained patents and had it all declared their property. Very unrelaxed – unenlightened, as we say nowadays. But we only understood all of this once digital space was completely imbued with it and lockdown had landlocked us, so to speak. You remember: Back then, we cut off all communication with the rest of the world, in order to rediscover the innocence of our desire. Be assured: We still are adventurers!

I guess that's what Old-Europeans think humor is. But you are ignoring the facts: you let yourselves go! You avoid tidying up your identity clusters and naively hope everything will be fine. I'm telling you: Your society is a loose cannon!

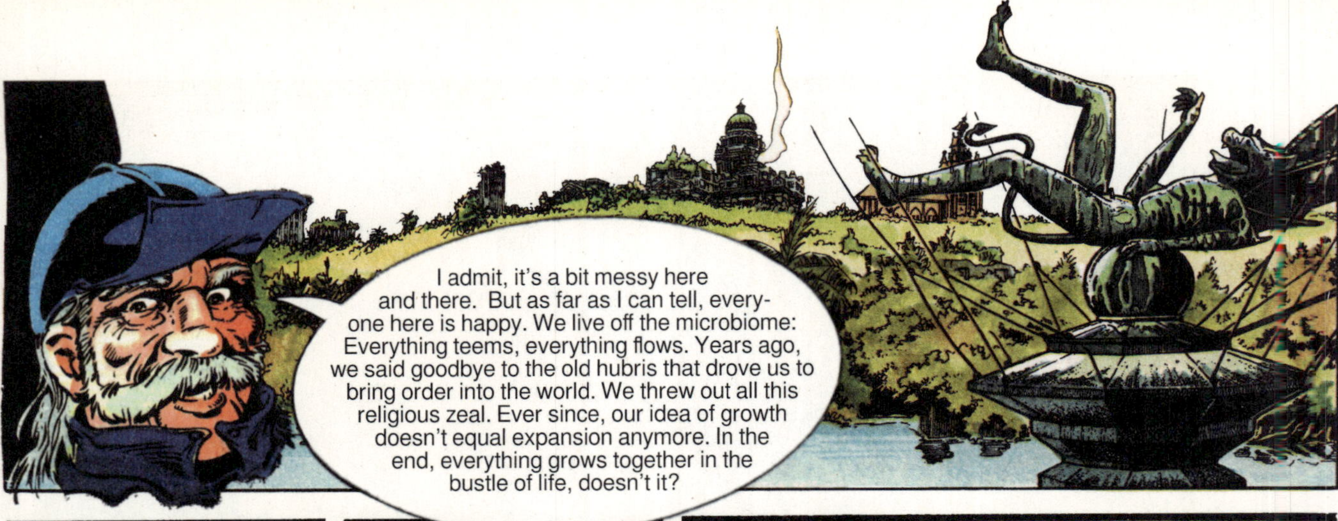

I admit, it's a bit messy here and there. But as far as I can tell, everyone here is happy. We live off the microbiome: Everything teems, everything flows. Years ago, we said goodbye to the old hubris that drove us to bring order into the world. We threw out all this religious zeal. Ever since, our idea of growth doesn't equal expansion anymore. In the end, everything grows together in the bustle of life, doesn't it?

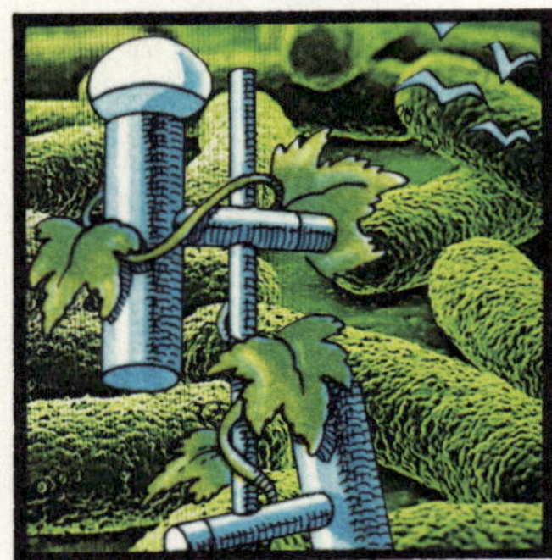

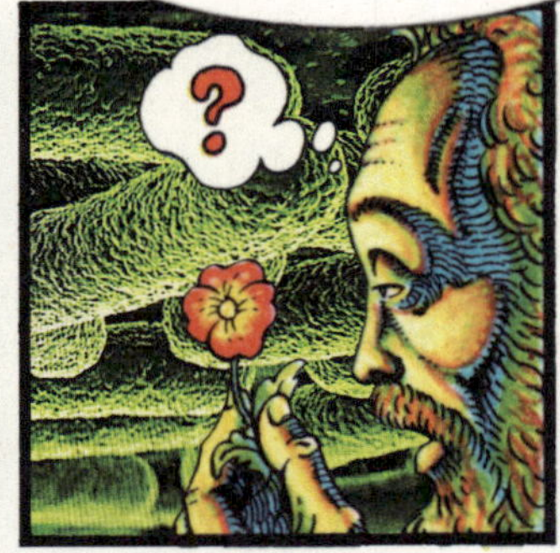

?

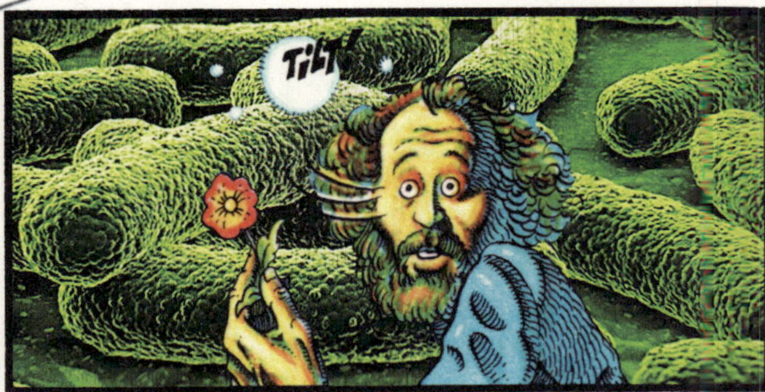

Tilt

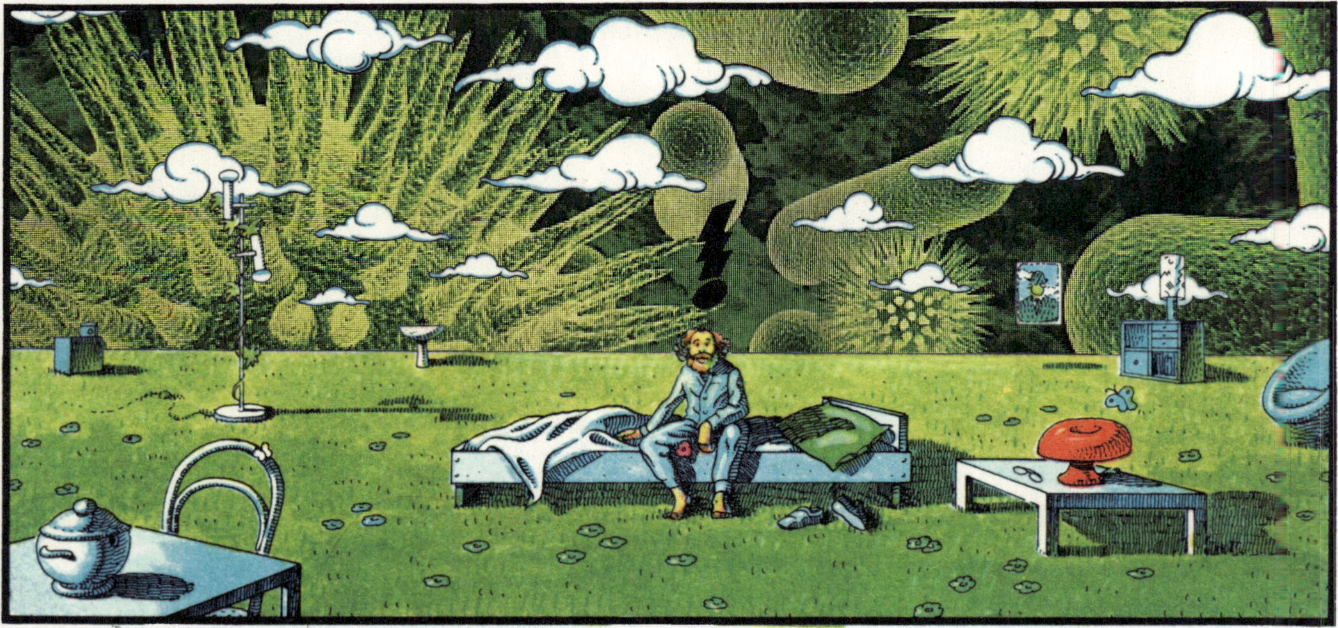

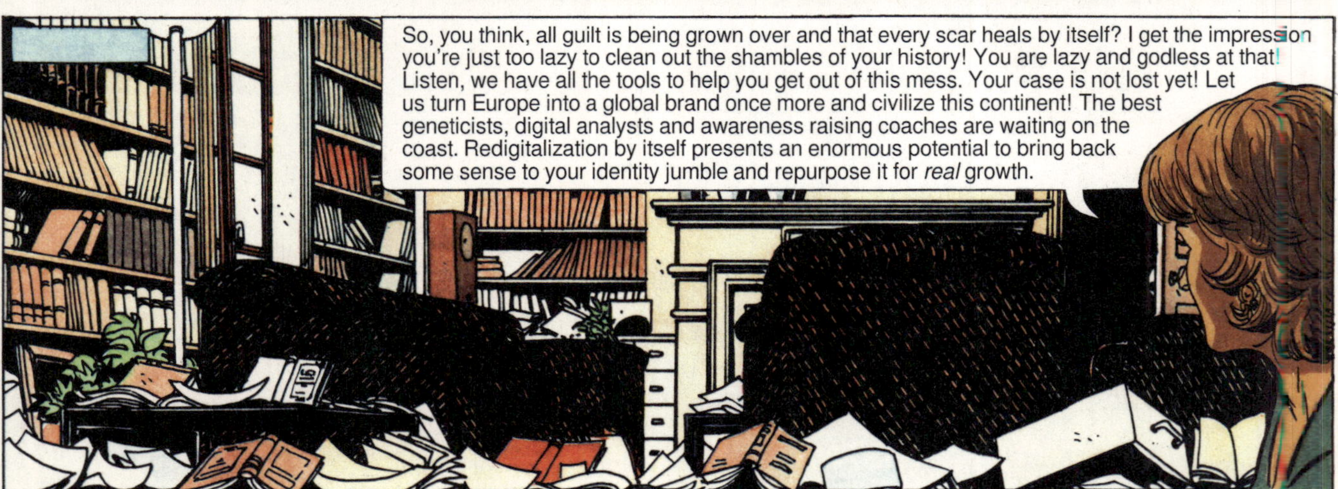

So, you think, all guilt is being grown over and that every scar heals by itself? I get the impression you're just too lazy to clean out the shambles of your history! You are lazy and godless at that! Listen, we have all the tools to help you get out of this mess. Your case is not lost yet! Let us turn Europe into a global brand once more and civilize this continent! The best geneticists, digital analysts and awareness raising coaches are waiting on the coast. Redigitalization by itself presents an enormous potential to bring back some sense to your identity jumble and repurpose it for *real* growth.

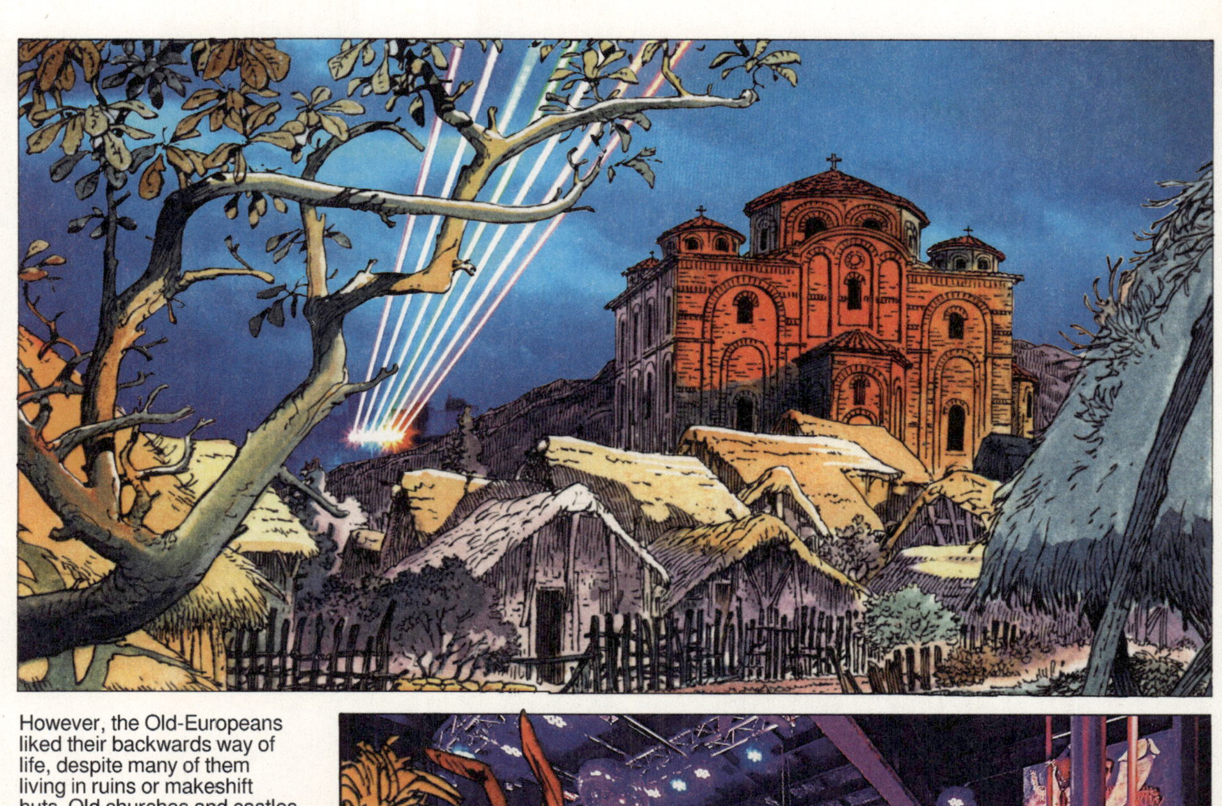

However, the Old-Europeans liked their backwards way of life, despite many of them living in ruins or makeshift huts. Old churches and castles were converted into temples of lust where countless festivities took place.

Besides the books and artistic endeavors that are hard to explain to outsiders, the playful eroticism taking place there was some of the last surviving proof of the Old-Europeans ingenuity. It kept them from instantly perishing under the weight of their peculiar idleness.
Euro-pessimism, that's what they called this withdrawn, shameless decadence.

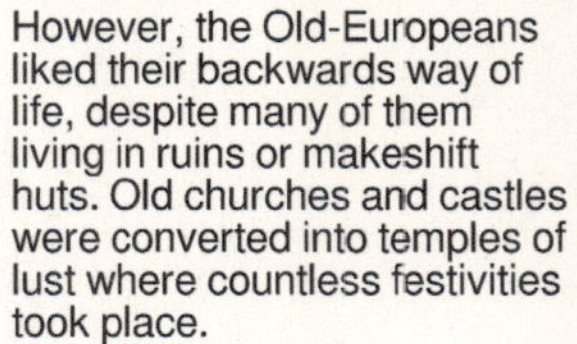

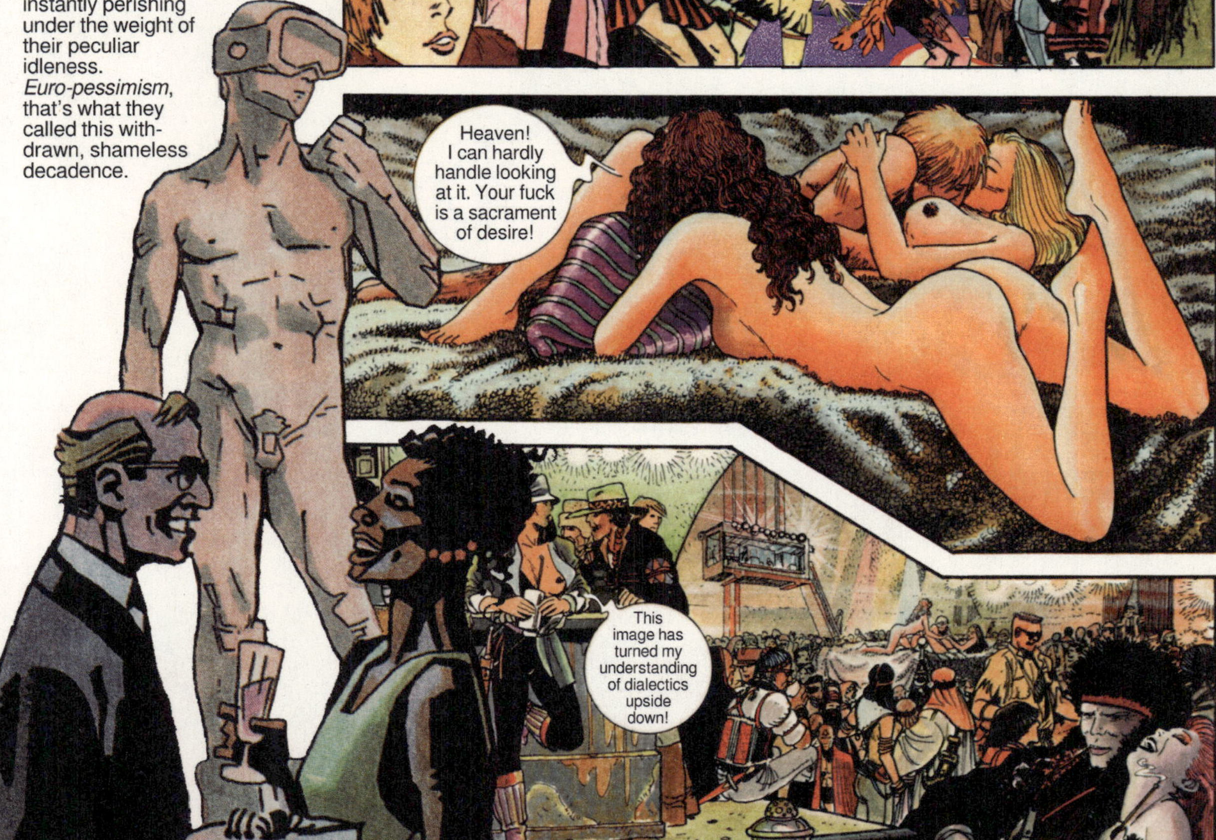

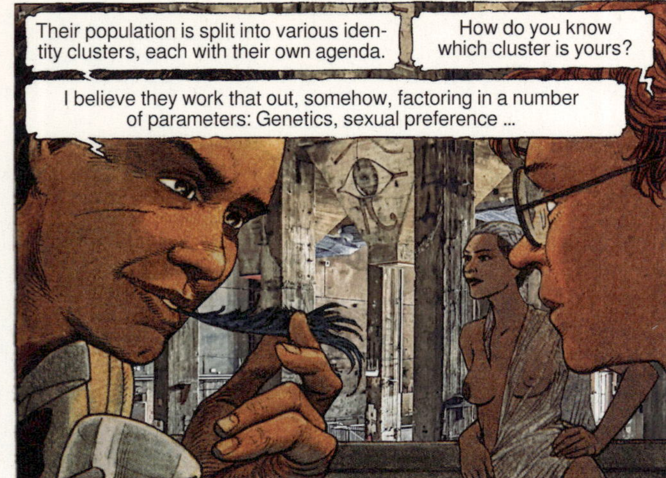

Their population is split into various identity clusters, each with their own agenda.
How do you know which cluster is yours?
I believe they work that out, somehow, factoring in a number of parameters: Genetics, sexual preference …

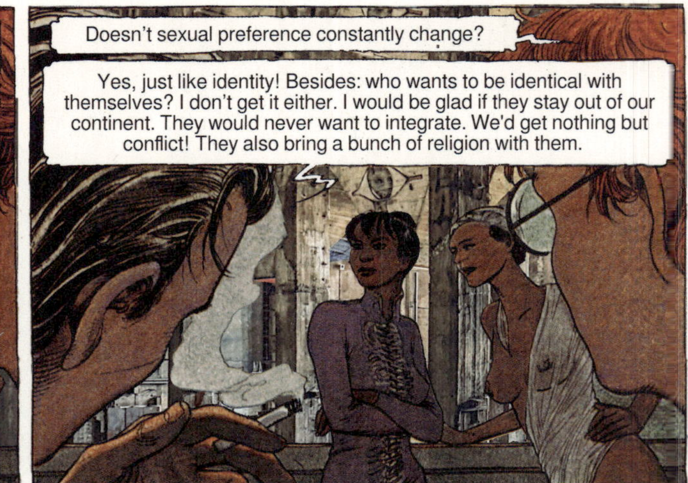

Doesn't sexual preference constantly change?
Yes, just like identity! Besides: who wants to be identical with themselves? I don't get it either. I would be glad if they stay out of our continent. They would never want to integrate. We'd get nothing but conflict! They also bring a bunch of religion with them.

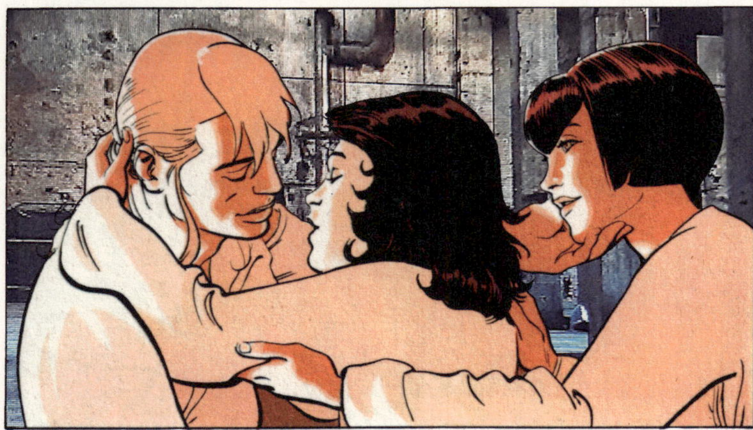

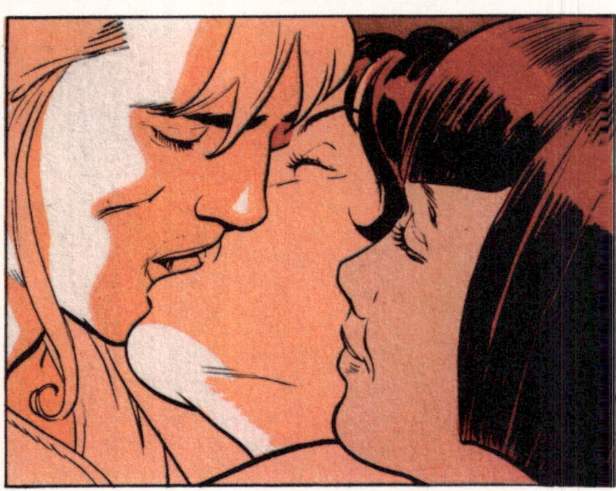

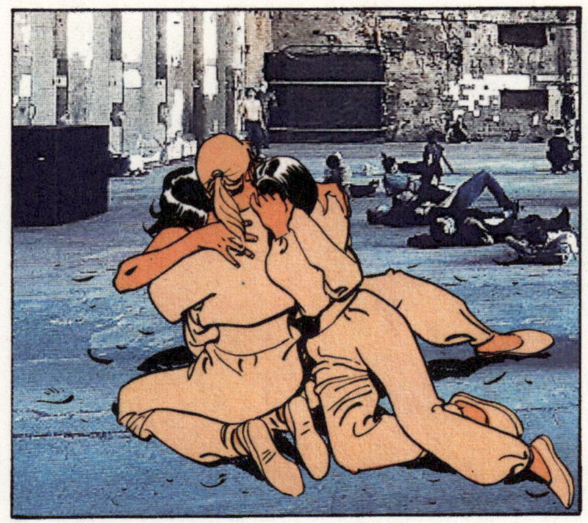

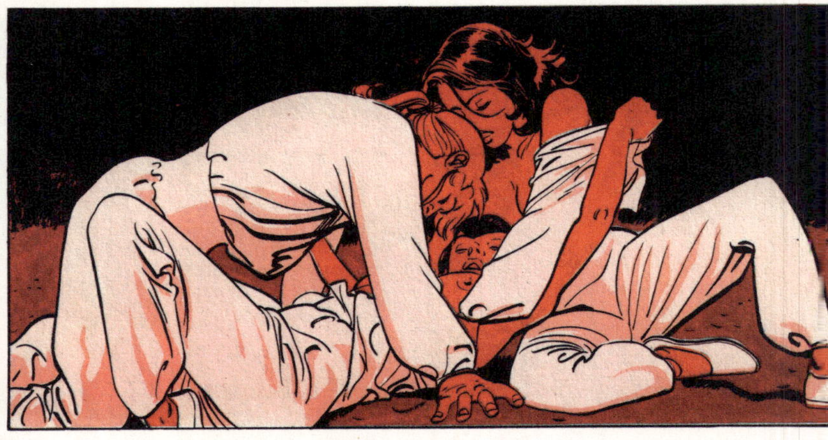

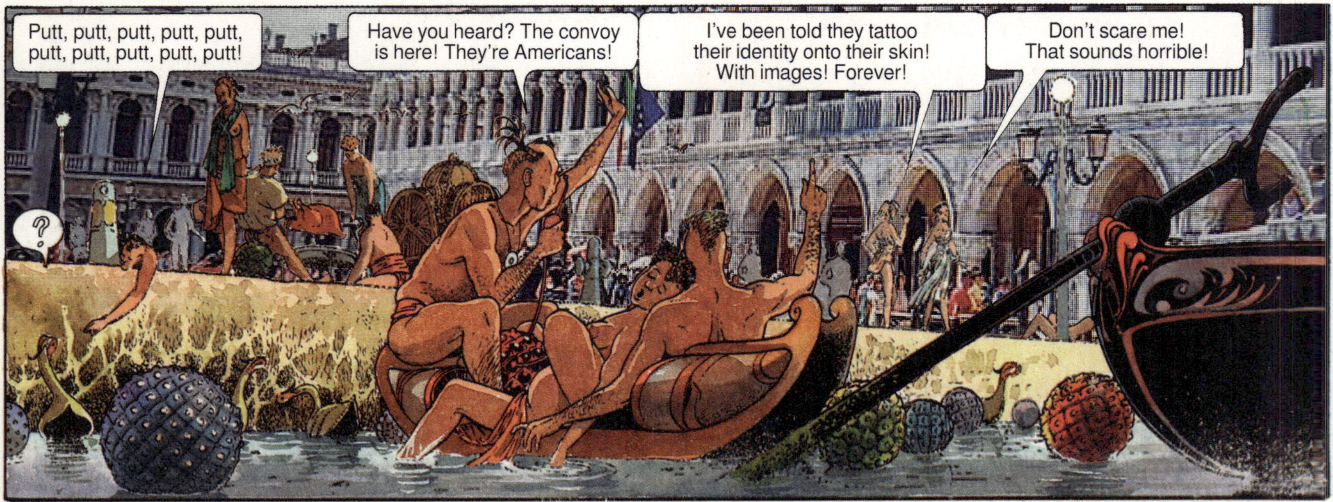

Putt, putt, putt, putt, putt, putt, putt, putt, putt, putt!
Have you heard? The convoy is here! They're Americans!
I've been told they tattoo their identity onto their skin! With images! Forever!
Don't scare me! That sounds horrible!

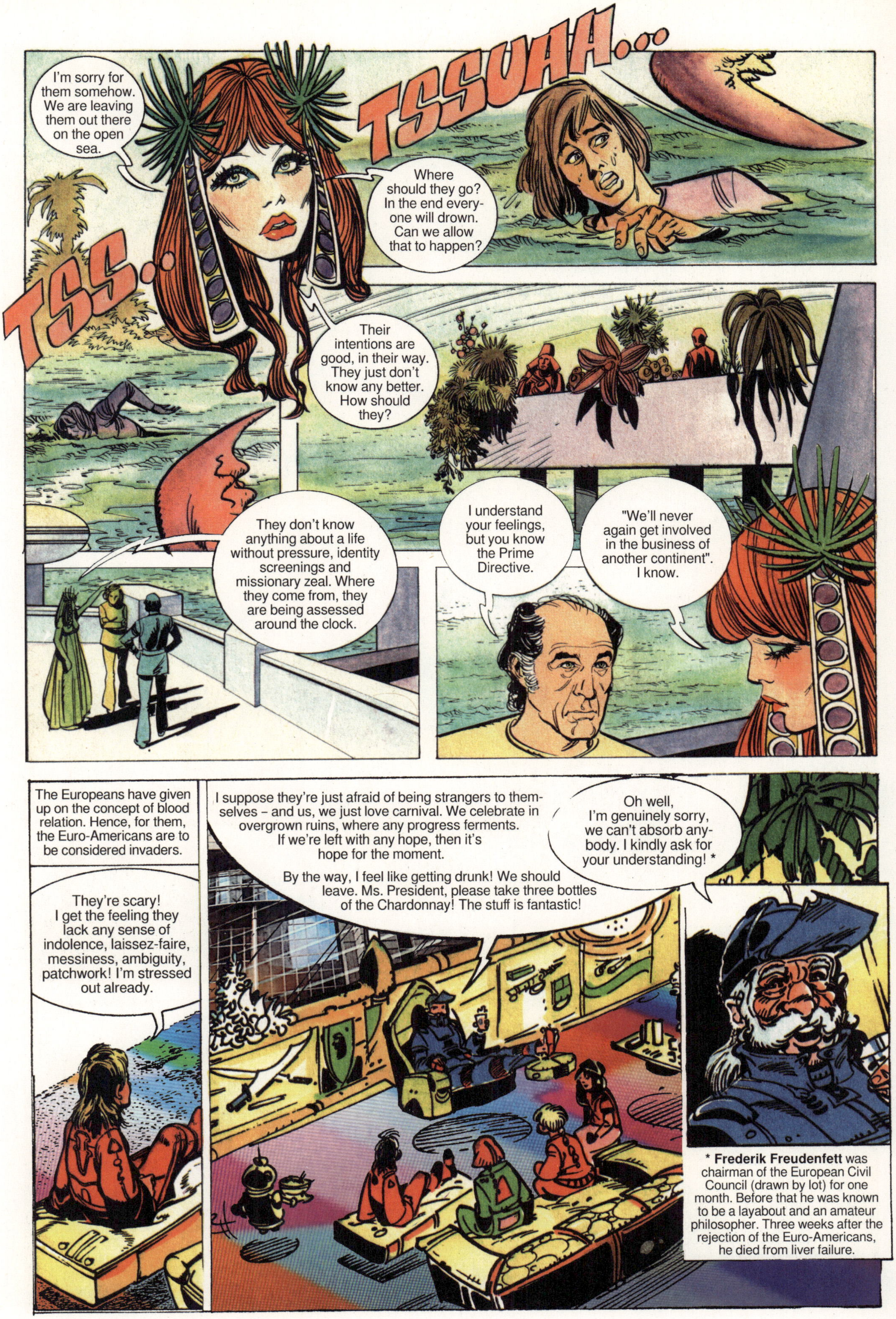

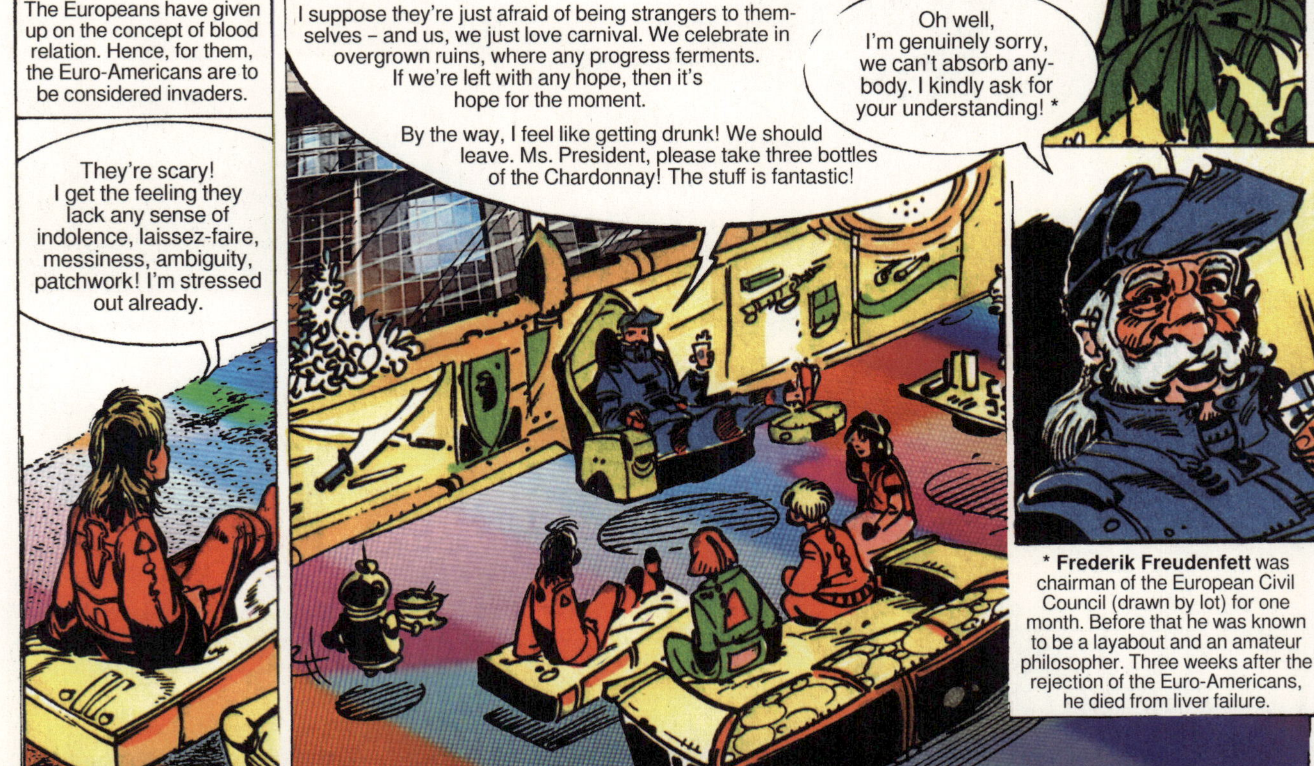

* **Frederik Freudenfett** was chairman of the European Civil Council (drawn by lot) for one month. Before that he was known to be a layabout and an amateur philosopher. Three weeks after the rejection of the Euro-Americans, he died from liver failure.

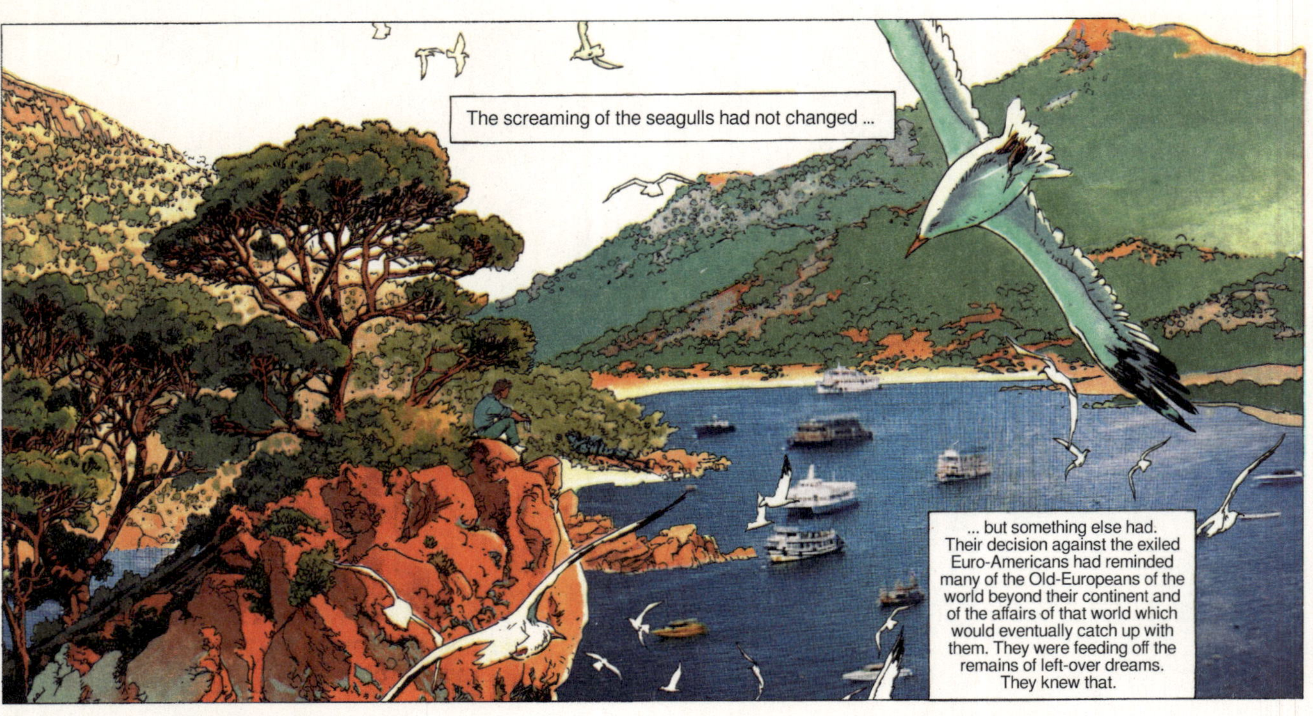

The screaming of the seagulls had not changed ...
... but something else had. Their decision against the exiled Euro-Americans had reminded many of the Old-Europeans of the world beyond their continent and of the affairs of that world which would eventually catch up with them. They were feeding off the remains of left-over dreams. They knew that.
Theirs was a retired civilization which had become mild when faced with its own contradictions. It wasn't doubt that made the round among them but a silent melancholy.

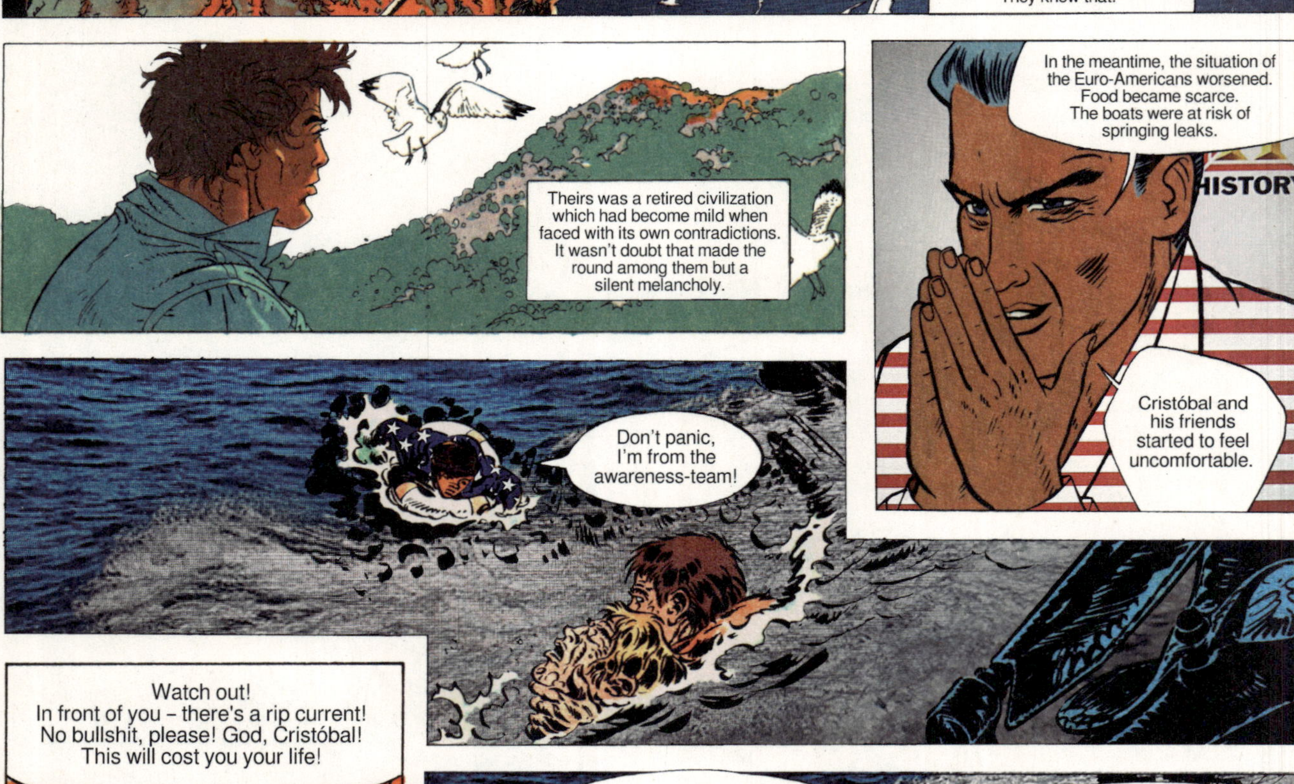

In the meantime, the situation of the Euro-Americans worsened. Food became scarce. The boats were at risk of springing leaks.
HISTORY
Cristóbal and his friends started to feel uncomfortable.
Don't panic, I'm from the awareness-team!

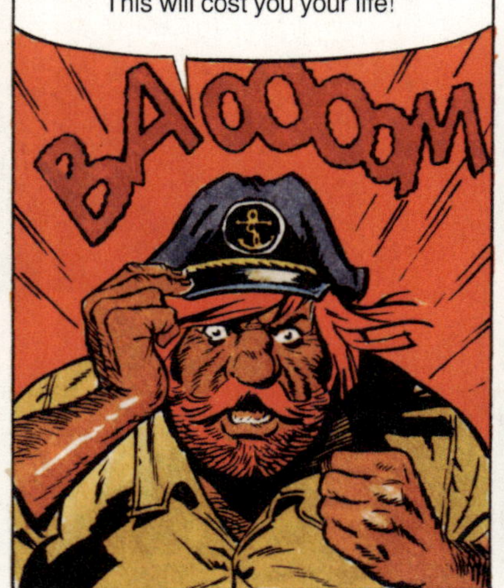

Watch out! In front of you – there's a rip current! No bullshit, please! God, Cristóbal! This will cost you your life!
BAOOOOM

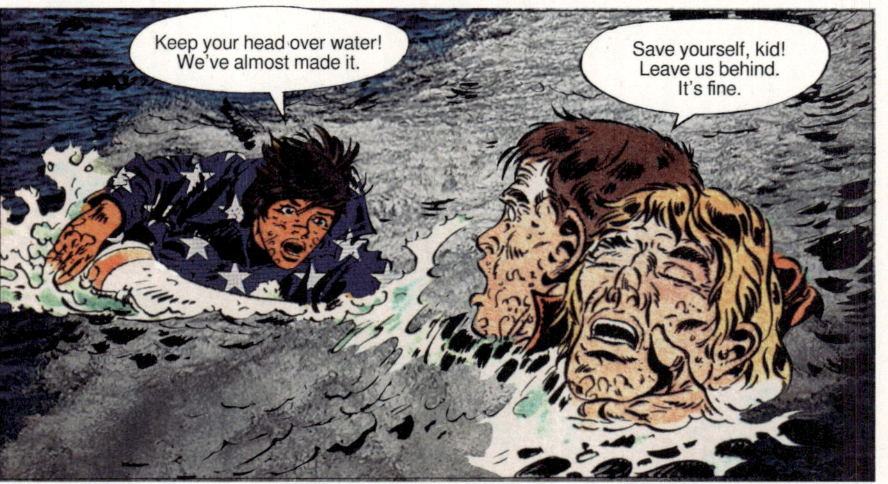

Keep your head over water! We've almost made it.
Save yourself, kid! Leave us behind. It's fine.

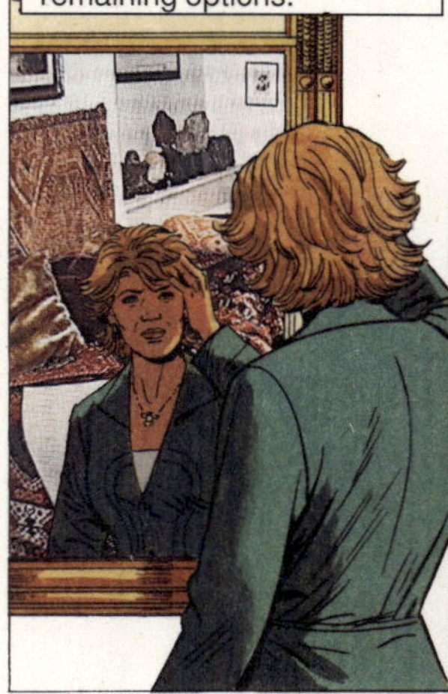

In the chill-out lounge of the European Civil Council, the delegation discussed their remaining options.

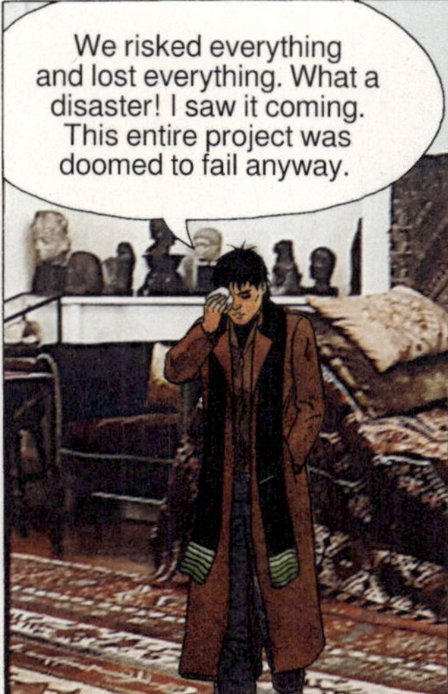

We risked everything and lost everything. What a disaster! I saw it coming. This entire project was doomed to fail anyway.

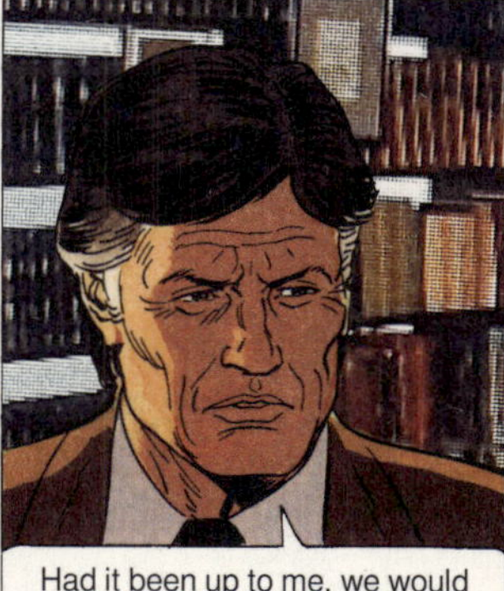

Had it been up to me, we would have never decolonized in such a grandiose manner. We should have colonized these Old-European cavemen the way it was done in the good old days. It could have even taken place without any military means.

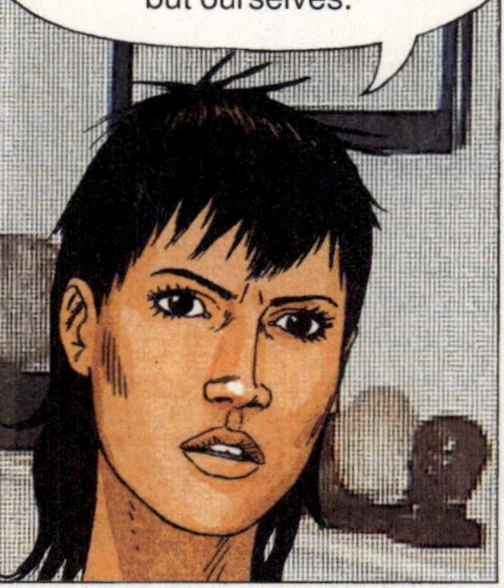

Puh! You were the one who kept crying about your colonial complex! It's too late anyway: we've left behind all our resources – we have nothing but ourselves.

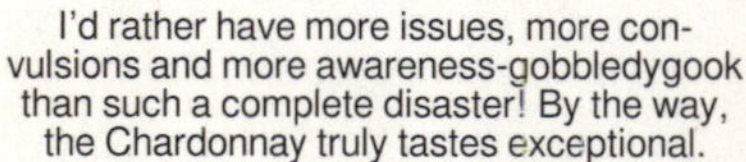

I'd rather have more issues, more convulsions and more awareness-gobbledygook than such a complete disaster! By the way, the Chardonnay truly tastes exceptional.

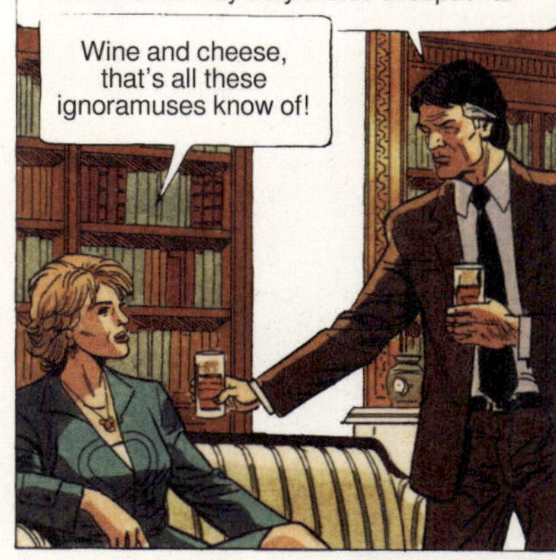

Wine and cheese, that's all these ignoramuses know of!

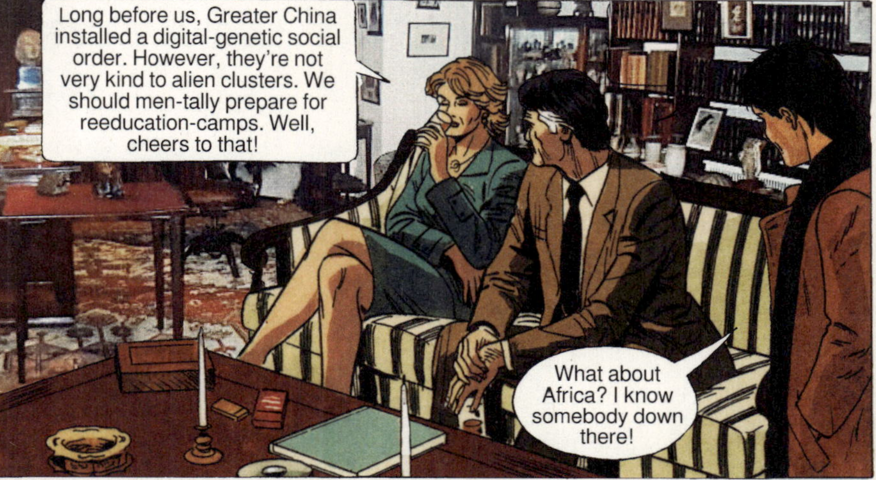

Long before us, Greater China installed a digital-genetic social order. However, they're not very kind to alien clusters. We should men-tally prepare for reeducation-camps. Well, cheers to that!
What about Africa? I know somebody down there!

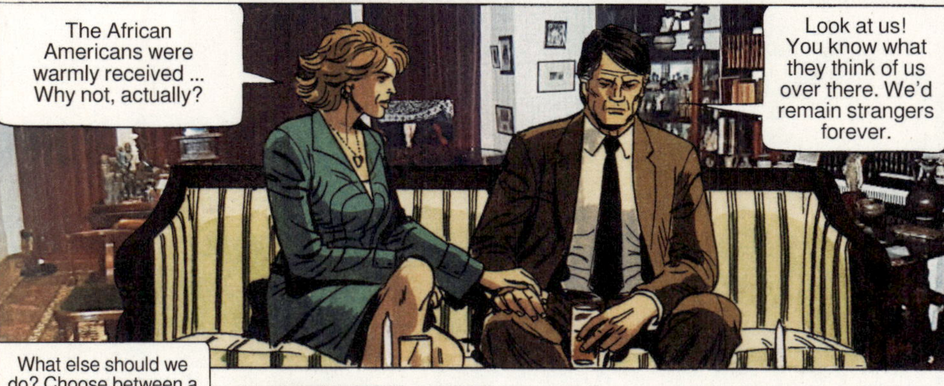

The African Americans were warmly received ... Why not, actually?
Look at us! You know what they think of us over there. We'd remain strangers forever.

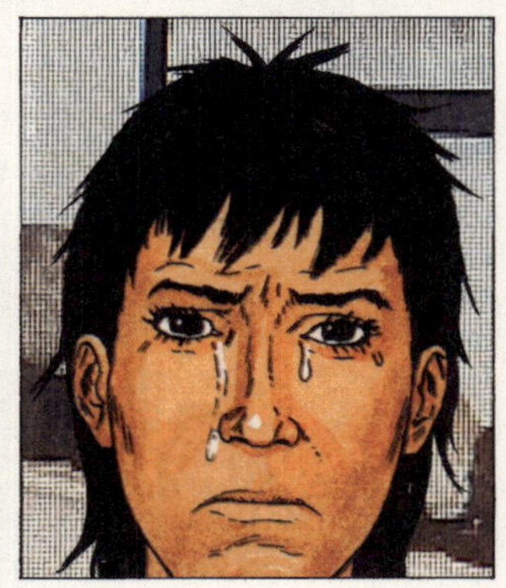

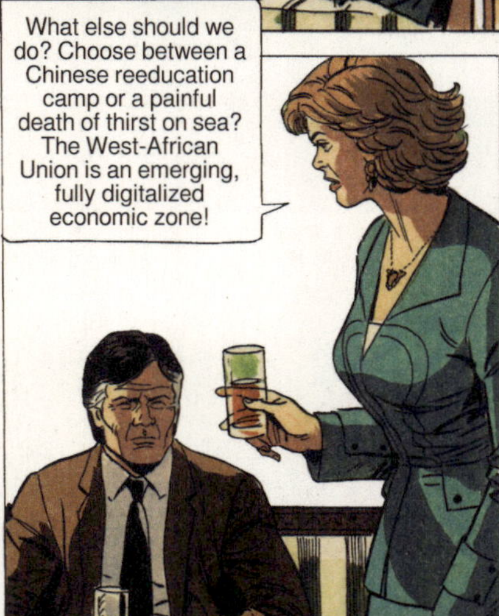

What else should we do? Choose between a Chinese reeducation camp or a painful death of thirst on sea? The West-African Union is an emerging, fully digitalized economic zone!

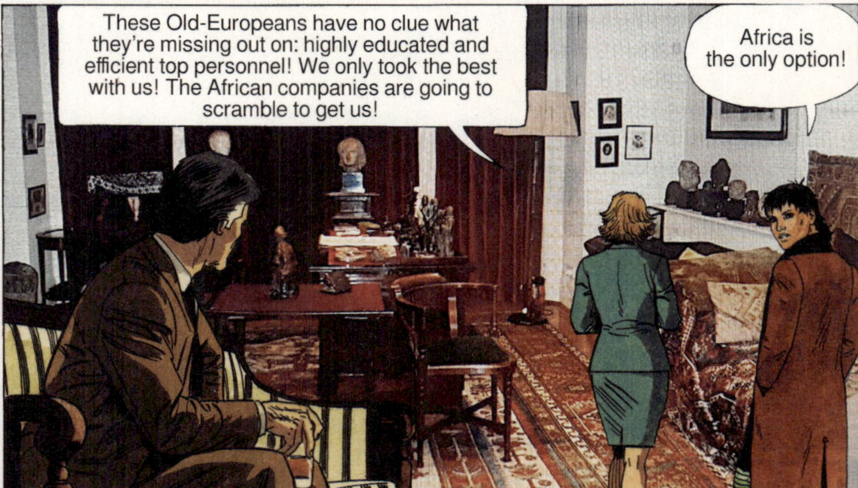

These Old-Europeans have no clue what they're missing out on: highly educated and efficient top personnel! We only took the best with us! The African companies are going to scramble to get us!
Africa is the only option!

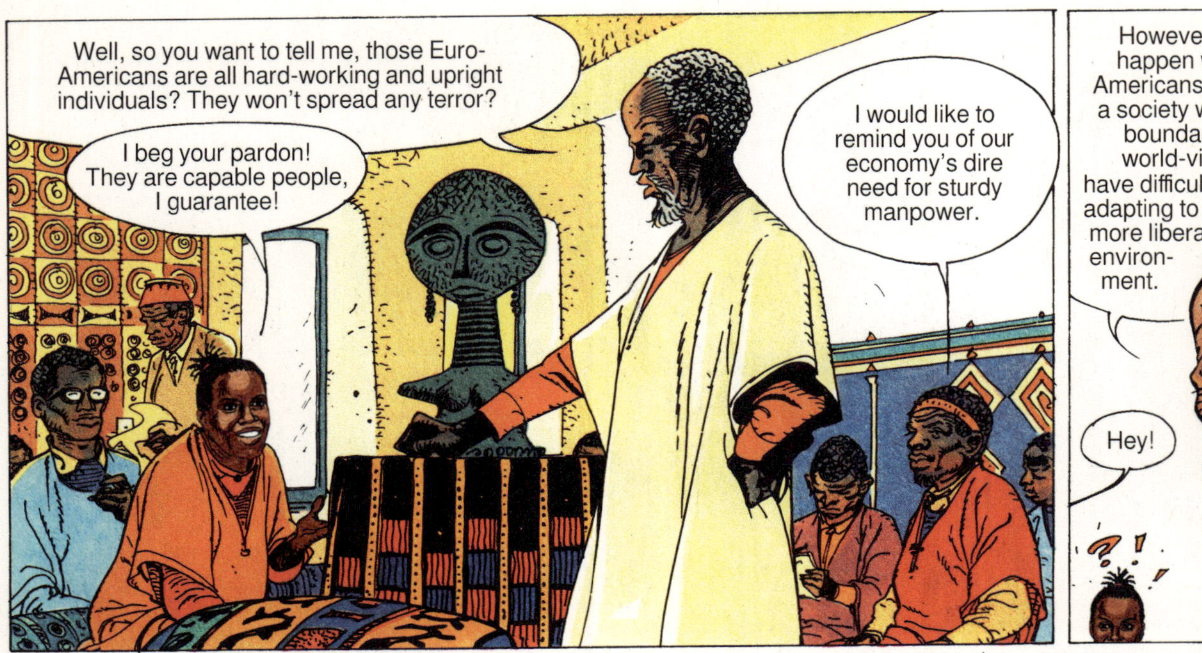

Well, so you want to tell me, those Euro-Americans are all hard-working and upright individuals? They won't spread any terror?
I beg your pardon! They are capable people, I guarantee!
I would like to remind you of our economy's dire need for sturdy manpower.

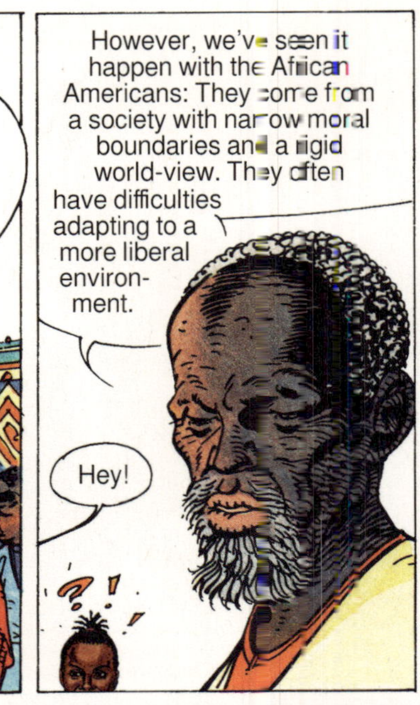

However, we've seen it happen with the African Americans: They come from a society with narrow moral boundaries and a rigid world-view. They often have difficulties adapting to a more liberal environment.
Hey!

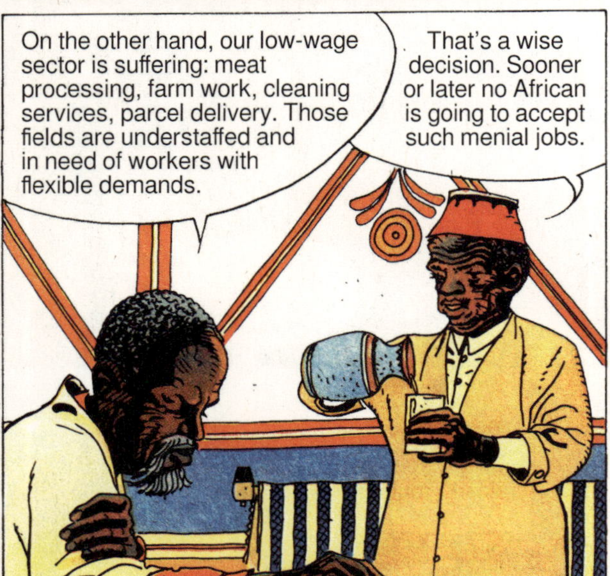

On the other hand, our low-wage sector is suffering: meat processing, farm work, cleaning services, parcel delivery. Those fields are understaffed and in need of workers with flexible demands.
That's a wise decision. Sooner or later no African is going to accept such menial jobs.

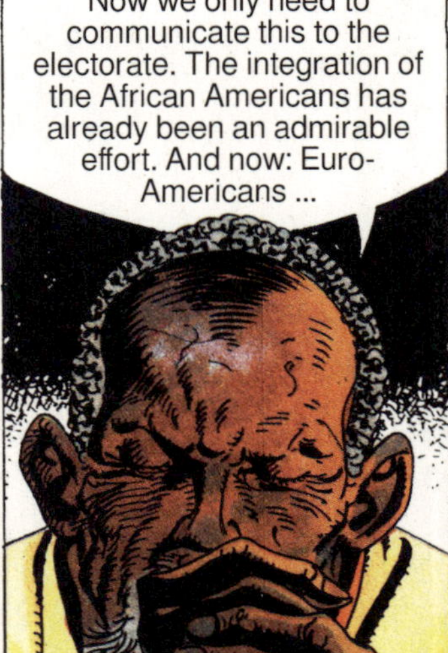

Now we only need to communicate this to the electorate. The integration of the African Americans has already been an admirable effort. And now: Euro-Americans ...

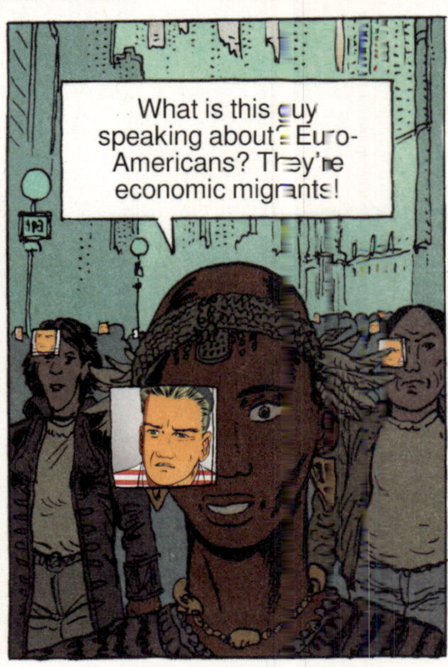

What is this guy speaking about? Euro-Americans? They're economic migrants!

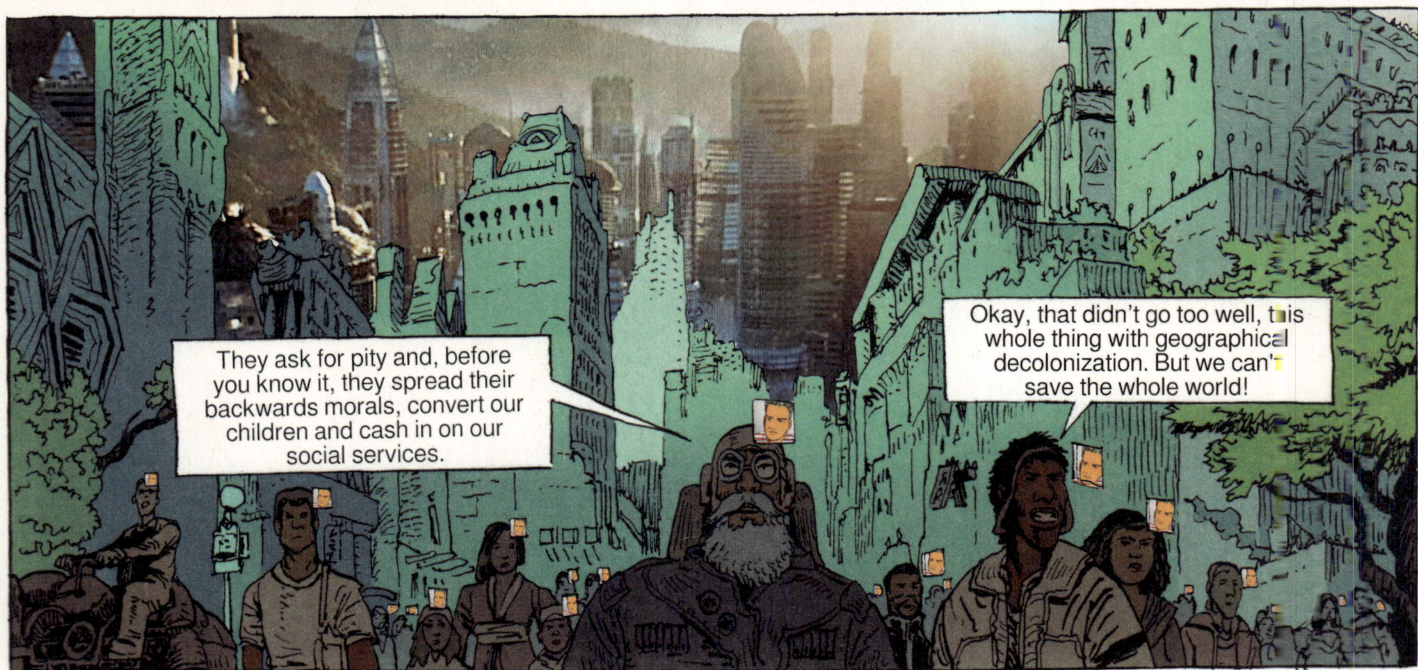

They ask for pity and, before you know it, they spread their backwards morals, convert our children and cash in on our social services.
Okay, that didn't go too well, this whole thing with geographical decolonization. But we can't save the whole world!